Economic Dimensions of Security in Central Asia

Sergej Mahnovski, Kamil Akramov,
Theodore Karasik

Prepared for the United States Air Force

PROJECT AIR FORCE

The research described in this report was sponsored by the United States Air Force under Contract F49642-01-C-0003. Further information may be obtained from the Strategic Planning Division, Directorate of Plans, Hq USAF.

Library of Congress Cataloging-in-Publication Data

Mahnovski, Sergej.
    Economic dimensions of security in Central Asia / Sergej Mahnovski, Kamil Akramov, Theodore Karasik.
        p. cm.
    "MG-417."
    Includes bibliographical references.
    ISBN 0-8330-3866-4 (pbk. : alk. paper)
    1. Asia, Central—Economic conditions—1991– 2. Asia, Central—Social conditions—1991– 3. Economic assistance, American—Asia, Central.
I. Akramov, Kamil. II. Karasik, Theodore William. III. Title.

HC420.3.M34 2006
330.958—dc22

                                                              2005030425

The RAND Corporation is a nonprofit research organization providing objective analysis and effective solutions that address the challenges facing the public and private sectors around the world. RAND's publications do not necessarily reflect the opinions of its research clients and sponsors.

RAND® is a registered trademark.

Published 2007 by the RAND Corporation
1776 Main Street, P.O. Box 2138, Santa Monica, CA 90407-2138
1200 South Hayes Street, Arlington, VA 22202-5050
4570 Fifth Avenue, Suite 600, Pittsburgh, PA 15213-2665
RAND URL: http://www.rand.org/
To order RAND documents or to obtain additional information, contact
Distribution Services: Telephone: (310) 451-7002
Fax: (310) 451-6915; Email: order@rand.org

Central Asia

Preface

This report assesses the economic dimensions of security in post-Soviet Central Asia and considers their implications for the role of the United States. The September 11, 2001, attacks on the United States led those in policymaking circles to realize that instability, failed and failing states, and economic and political underdevelopment present security concerns not just to the states that suffer directly from these problems but to the global community as a whole. From this perspective, political, social, and economic trends in Central Asia merit attention.

The report should be of interest to policymakers and analysts involved in international security and U.S. foreign policy. The analysis in this report is informed by a year-long research effort, which included travel to the region and extensive interviews with U.S., regional, and global specialists, government officials, and others. It involved a multidisciplinary team of researchers who sought to combine their understanding of politics, economics, and military strategic analysis to bring fresh perspectives to the questions at hand.

The research reported here was sponsored by AF/A5X and conducted within the Strategy and Doctrine Program of RAND Project AIR FORCE. Comments are welcome and may be directed to the authors and to Andrew Hoehn, director of Project AIR FORCE's Strategy and Doctrine Program. Until late 2003, Edward Harshberger, then–director of the Strategy and Doctrine Program, provided leadership and support. Until late 2004, acting director Alan Vick oversaw the completion of this effort. Research for this report, which was undertaken as part of a project entitled "The USAF in Central Asia: Issues and Prospects," was largely completed in late 2003, although some updates were made as late as September 2005.

RAND Project AIR FORCE

RAND Project AIR FORCE (PAF), a division of the RAND Corporation, is the U.S. Air Force's federally funded research and development center for studies and analyses. PAF provides the Air Force with independent analyses of policy alternatives affecting the development, employment, combat readiness, and support of current and future aerospace forces. Research is conducted in four programs: Aerospace Force Development; Manpower, Personnel, and Training; Resource Management; and Strategy and Doctrine.

Additional information about PAF is available on our Web site at http://www.rand.org/paf.

Contents

Figures

Tables

Summary

Objective

This report assesses the political implications of economic and related social problems in the five post-Soviet Central Asian states of Kazakhstan, Kyrgyzstan, Tajikistan, Turkmenistan, and Uzbekistan. It also suggests U.S. policy measures that would help address these problems, consistent with broader U.S. goals in the region. The September 11, 2001, attacks on the United States led those in policymaking circles to realize that instability, failed and failing states, and economic and political underdevelopment present security concerns not just to the states that suffer directly from these problems but to the global community as a whole. From this perspective, political, social, and economic trends in Central Asia merit attention.

The Implications of Economic and Social Problems for Stability

Economic development will play a pivotal role in the social and political evolution of post-Soviet Central Asia. Despite the promise of abundant natural resources and increased international attention in the wake of Operation Enduring Freedom, the people of Central Asia face an uncertain future. U.S. policymakers are increasingly acknowledging that the security challenges in the region may well include the effects of widespread dissatisfaction with economic policies and corruption, the growth of organized crime networks, and deteriorating social conditions. The relationship between economic policies and political developments in Central Asia is not straightforward. However, the record suggests that a lack of economic opportunities can play a major role in fostering instability and, potentially, conflict, particularly when it is compounded by perceptions of government mismanagement and political disenfranchisement. As the United States defines its policies toward the states of Central Asia, it must view economic development in the region as itself a long-term security concern. Popular discontent in Kyrgyzstan and Uzbekistan in early 2005 underscore these issues and their importance.

Uzbekistan, the most populous and geographically central state in Central Asia, has emerged as the central player in the prospects for regional development and long-term economic growth. Uzbekistan is facing a transition period where policy choices regarding economic and political liberalization directly affect its ability to alleviate the discontent associated with poverty and unemployment. These choices will have implications outside Uzbekistan and could further contribute to the division of Central Asia into a relatively wealthy Kazakhstan and a poor, fractious, southern flank.

Economic Trends

From an economic perspective, the states of Central Asia may be characterized as much by their differences as by their similarities.

After a difficult market transition period in the early 1990s, Kazakhstan has posted impressive economic growth figures in recent years, largely as a result of its relatively favorable geographic position, billions of dollars of foreign direct investment (FDI) in its oil and gas sectors, and liberal economic policies. Kazakhstan has accounted for almost 50 percent of the region's total gross domestic product (GDP) and 85 percent of cumulative FDI since independence and is more closely linked with Russia in terms of infrastructure and trade than with the rest of Central Asia. (See pp. 7–8.)

Uzbekistan and Turkmenistan, both endowed with substantial natural resources, have failed to implement any significant political and economic reform measures. Despite their economic potential, they have attracted the lowest FDI in the region, relative to the size of their economies, because of major state interventions in their economies and an unfavorable investment climate. Turkmenistan, a major natural gas producer, will likely remain an isolated, command economy, linked to the rest of the region primarily through natural gas trade. The prospects for Uzbekistan's long-term economic growth and stability remain uncertain and will depend on the regime's approach to balancing internal security challenges and political and economic liberalization. (See p. 8.)

Tajikistan and Kyrgyzstan, the smallest economies of the region, remain highly dependent on foreign assistance and an undiversified trade structure, which has made them highly sensitive to fluctuations in commodity prices. However, both have a relatively favorable track record with international donors, who are actively involved in infrastructure projects and debt restructuring, which will free up money for greater investment spending. (See p. 8.)

Sectoral Trends

The Caspian Sea region promises to become an important second-tier supplier of oil to the world market and a major regional supplier of natural gas over the next several decades. Hydrocarbon exports will be a critical source of government revenues in Kazakhstan and Turkmenistan. On balance, the existence of significant hydrocarbon and mineral reserves gives Kazakhstan and Turkmenistan an opportunity to bolster their geopolitical relevance and economic development. Although they are only in the early stages of their post-Soviet hydrocarbon boom, Kazakhstan, Turkmenistan, and Uzbekistan already suffer from some of the classic institutional pathologies evident in other resource-rich regimes, such as off-budget petroleum (and other mineral) accounts, and oil and gas ministries that wield disproportionate influence over other elements of the government. (See pp. 36–47.)

However, the prospects for foreign direct investment outside the energy and mining industries are bleak, largely because of an unfavorable and, in most cases, corrupt business environment, but also because of decaying infrastructure and the remote, landlocked geographic position of the resources.

Poverty is disproportionately severe in the countryside, and the agricultural sector is the chief employer of the rural populations of Central Asia. However, agricultural productivity is constrained by major state intervention in both the input and output markets and by severe water shortages, particularly in the cotton and grain-growing areas in Uzbekistan and Turkmenistan. Severe unemployment has led to a northerly seasonal migration from all the Central Asian states to Russia and Kazakhstan. Tajikistan grows less than one-half of its food needs and remains dependent on food aid and imports from abroad. The lack of arable land and farm credit for crops other than cotton has discouraged private investment in other agricultural commodities in Tajikistan and malnourishment will remain a challenge there.

Water is a key security issue, particularly for Turkmenistan and Uzbekistan, which have a high demand for irrigation water to support their over-leveraged agricultural industries. Although there is little prospect for a multilateral solution to water allocation in the region, the prospects for a "water war" are slim. Most conflicts over water have been local, with little or no ethnic dimension. (See pp. 29–36.)

Social Trends

Economic development depends on a healthy, well-educated, and capable workforce. The deterioration of the health care system in Central Asia has cast doubt on the ability of the region to confront some of the new health care challenges it faces, such as HIV/AIDS. Although Central Asia still enjoys a high level of literacy for its level of income, the steady deterioration of the educational system over the past decade has increased the mismatch between the skill sets of young Central Asians and those demanded by the global market, potentially retarding long-term economic growth. This is especially severe in Turkmenistan, where educational standards have deteriorated significantly in recent years. (See pp. 52–54.)

Trade in illicit drugs has empowered organized crime networks and negatively affected the health and personal security of citizens in

Central Asia. There has been a discernible shift in drug trafficking of Afghan opium from traditional Iranian routes toward Central Asia in recent years. The introduction of heroin use by intravenous injection has increased the spread of HIV/AIDS in the region, which threatens to become a public health crisis in the future. The nature and scope of the organized crime networks and their possible connections, in some cases, with the regimes in Central Asia are very difficult to measure. (See pp. 49–52, 54–59.)

Foreign Assistance In Central Asia

The prevailing wisdom since the collapse of the Soviet Union has been that the presence of Western political and economic entities would have a beneficial effect on democratization and economic reform. However, the record of international financial institutions, multinational corporations, and international nongovernmental organizations has been decidedly mixed in Central Asia, and particularly discouraging in Uzbekistan and Turkmenistan. (See pp. 61–70.)

If one goal of international assistance is to help a country eventually access the international private capital market, Kazakhstan can be regarded as a success. Today, Kazakhstan has access to international financial markets, enjoys fairly well developed domestic financial markets and institutions, and has posted impressive economic growth figures over the past several years. Donors have helped Kyrgyzstan and Tajikistan avert possible humanitarian crises and, some would argue, implement preliminary democratic and market reforms. However, both are expected to remain highly dependent on foreign aid and a very limited slate of export commodities. The international community has had very little success in promoting economic or political reform in Uzbekistan and Turkmenistan and may, in fact, have inadvertently delayed it by lending to them in the 1990s.

U.S. Policy Options

The United States must balance its strategic military relationships in the region with the potentially disparate goal of fostering domestic reform and sustainable economic development. Economic development will be crucial to long-term development in Central Asia and broader U.S. interests in the region. However, it is unclear whether these states have the institutional capacity to implement sound and lasting economic policies and whether the United States and the international community are offering the appropriate combination of incentives to enable this. One challenge for the United States and the international community is to offer sound policies despite the opaqueness of the internal dynamics of the region's regimes, particularly in Uzbekistan and Turkmenistan. As the United States clarifies its long-term military relationships and commitments, it should consider the region's economic development as a long-term security concern itself. (See pp. 71–73.)

Several issues merit attention in the discussion of economic dimensions of security in Central Asia:

- Central Asia will increasingly diversify its economic and military relationships with neighbors such as Russia, China, and Iran, potentially crowding out U.S. influence in the region. The United States does not have a direct, compelling economic interest in Central Asia outside Kazakhstan's oil sector. Nor does most of Central Asia depend on direct economic assistance from or trade with the United States. Thus, Central Asia's economic future lies primarily within its own neighborhood. However, U.S. actions may have an effect on shaping the involvement of Central Asia's neighbors in the region. Insofar as the other regional powers share the U.S. goals of fostering development in the region, they should be engaged. In particular, cooperation with Russia may be crucial.
- Regime change in the region may occur with little warning and in spite of the efforts of the United States. If U.S. policymakers decide to maintain a military presence there, it may be necessary

to consider a wider range of approaches that lower the risk of long-term denial of access and perceptions of the United States as a regime patron. Although some have argued that a U.S. military presence could be used as a vehicle for encouraging domestic reform, the record to date provides little grounds for optimism. At a minimum, a lower-profile presence and hedging strategies should be part of U.S. strategic planning.

- A "nuanced" approach may be necessary in dealing with the more authoritarian regimes in Central Asia. The reality of governance in the region is that domestic policies are often the outcome of complex interactions among the elite stakeholders within the regime rather than of a centralized decision process. Although human-rights concerns may test the U.S. goal of promoting foreign policy at the intersection of our "vital interest and deepest beliefs," disengagement from Central Asia may compromise U.S. ability to attain overarching goals in the region. Policymakers should consider the costs and benefits of engaging alternative power centers within and outside of these regimes, possibly enlisting the support of other regional powers where common ground can be found.

- Economic and military assistance to the region should be more sharply focused to avoid the highest risk outcomes. In particular, failed state scenarios for Uzbekistan would result in major regional problems that would undermine broader U.S. goals, such as counterterror and counternarcotics strategies. However, policies that may be critical to stability, such as agricultural reform and free trade, remain important domestic political decisions and thus beyond the direct influence of the United States or multilateral institutions. Although a portfolio approach to assistance in the region has merit, a greater focus of diplomatic capital and economic resources on specific issues, such as political liberalization, may be necessary.

In conclusion, economic development will be crucial to the future of Central Asia and broader U.S. interests in the region. Although there are indications that the states of the region recognize this, it is unclear whether they have the institutional capacity to implement sound and lasting economic policies and whether the United States and the international community are offering the appropriate combination of incentives to enable this. The United States has limited ability or interest in becoming a regime patron but still may play a significant role in shaping the prospects for development in the region by influencing the nature and pace of political and economic reform, realizing that the principles and interests behind U.S. involvement are more enduring than any single regime is likely to be.

Acknowledgments

No effort of this scope can be carried out without significant assistance. The RAND research team, which includes, in addition to the authors of this report, Edwin S. Blasi, Rollie Lal, Olga Oliker, David A. Shlapak, and Prerna Singh, wants first of all to thank our project monitors at AF/A5X, in particular Colonel Anthony Hinen, Colonel Donald Jordan, Major General Michael Gould, Lieutenant Colonel (ret.) John Jerakis, and Lieutenant Colonel (ret.) Lon Stonebraker, who helped guide this research.

We are also grateful to colleagues at the Office of the Secretary of Defense, the Joint Staff, the Defense Intelligence Agency, Central Command, Central Command Air Forces, and European Command who helped us expand our knowledge and supported us at home and in the field. In addition, staff at the State Department, the Central Intelligence Agency, the Defense Intelligence Agency, the National Security Council, the U.S. Agency for International Development, the Department of Commerce (including the Business Information Service for the Newly Independent States), and the U.S. Treasury were generous with their time and their insights as were Ambassador Joseph Hulings, Robinder Bhatty, Daniel Burghardt, Colonel Jon E. Chicky, Katherine Hardin, and Scott Horton. Philip Micklin, emeritus professor of geography at Western Michigan University, provided insights on water resources in Central Asia. We learned a great deal from workshops and meetings facilitated by the Eurasia Group, DFI International, the Joint Staff, and the World Policy Institute Forum. RAND staff who played critical roles in the research effort were

Negeen Pegahi, Suzannah Sennetti, and Keith Crane. Vazha Nadare-ishvili provided his expertise on the view from the Caucasus.

We are pleased to acknowledge the efforts of all who enhanced this report's quality: Keith Crane and Theresa Sabonis-Helft provided excellent reviews, Patricia Bedrosian and Jane Siegel offered valuable editorial assistance, and Robert Ellenson and Julie McNall contrib-uted valuable comments. We are grateful for their time and effort. Although we have taken their comments into account in revising this book, none of them bears responsibility for any of the judgments or estimates we have made.

We are particularly grateful to the staffs of the U.S. embassies in Turkmenistan, Uzbekistan, and Kazakhstan, both past and present, and most especially to the defense attaché offices in each of these countries, where we were very warmly welcomed.

We are grateful to a number of representatives of embassy staffs, in the United States and abroad. In Washington, staff at the embas-sies of Turkey, Uzbekistan, Turkmenistan, and Kyrgyzstan deserve special thanks. In the region, we spoke to representatives at embassies of the Russian Federation, Turkey, China, and Iran, and we are grate-ful to all of them for their time and insights. We also spoke to a broad range of officials, business people, and specialists in the course of our travels and we want to extend our thanks to them.

Sarah Harting, Madeline Taylor, Miriam Schafer, Terri Perkins, and Colleen O'Connor made our efforts flow smoothly with their capable administrative support. RAND library staff including Roberta Shanman, Kristin McCool, Richard Bancroft, and Leroy Reyes were essential in collecting data and information relevant for our analysis.

Although the content of the report reflects the observations and opinions of those people interviewed, the authors accept the respon-sibility for the way those views are expressed in these pages.

Abbreviations

ADB	Asian Development Bank
AmCham	American Chamber of Commerce in Uzbekistan
bbl	barrel
bcm	billion cubic meters
BISNIS	Business Information Service for the Newly Independent States
BP	British Petroleum
BTC	Baku-Tbilisi-Ceyhan
CAR	Central Asian Republics
CBT	Central Bank of Turkmenistan
CENTAF	Central Command Air Forces
CENTCOM	Central Command
CentGas	Central Asian Gas
CIS	Commonwealth of Independent States
CNPC	China National Petroleum Corporation
CPC	Caspian Pipeline Consortium
EBRD	European Bank for Reconstruction and Development
EU	European Union

EUCOM	European Command
Eximbank	Export-Import Bank
FDI	foreign direct investment
FPS	Federal Border Service
FY	fiscal year
GDP	gross domestic product
GE	General Electric
GNI	Gross National Income
HuT	Hizb-ut Tahrir
ICG	International Crisis Group
IFI	International Financial Institution
ILO	International Labour Organization
IMF	International Monetary Fund
IMU	Islamic Movement of Uzbekistan
INBC	International Narcotics Control Board
INGO	International Non-Governmental Organization
IOM	International Organization for Migration
ITEC	Indian Technical and Economic Cooperation
KEGOC	Kazakhstan Electrical Grid Operating Company
kWh	kilowatt-hour
LNG	liquefied natural gas
MMBtu	million British thermal units
MNC	multinational corporation
NATO	North Atlantic Treaty Organization
NGO	nongovernmental organization
NWFP	North West Frontier Province

OEF	Operation Enduring Freedom
OIF	Operation Iraqi Freedom
OPEC	Organization of the Petroleum Exporting Countries
OPIC	Overseas Private Investment Corporation
OSCE	Organization for Security and Co-operation in Europe
PAF	Project AIR FORCE
PPP	Purchasing Power Parity
PSA	production-sharing agreement
SDR	Special Drawing Right
SME	small- and medium-sized enterprises
TAP	Trans-Afghan Pipeline
tcf	thousand cubic feet
Tcf	trillion cubic feet
TEA	total economic activity
UAE	United Arab Emirates
UES	Unified Energy Systems
UK	United Kingdom
UN	United Nations
UNCTAD	United Nations Conference on Trade and Development
UNODC	United Nations Office of Drug and Crime
USAF	United States Air Force
USAID	U.S. Agency for International Development
WMD	weapons of mass destruction
WTO	World Trade Organization

CHAPTER ONE

Introduction

This report assesses the economic dimensions of security in post-Soviet Central Asia and considers their implications for the role of the United States. The September 11, 2001, attacks on the United States led those in policymaking circles to realize that instability, failed and failing states, and economic and political underdevelopment present security concerns not just to the states that suffer directly from these problems but to the global community as a whole. From this perspective, political, social, and economic trends in Central Asia merit attention.

Economic development will play a pivotal role in the social and political stability of post-Soviet Central Asia. Despite the promise of abundant natural resources and increased international attention in the wake of Operation Enduring Freedom, the people of Central Asia face an uncertain future. Policymakers are increasingly acknowledging that the security challenges in the region, which have traditionally been articulated as the threat from foreign insurgents, may also include the potentially destabilizing effects of widespread dissatisfaction with economic policies and corruption, the growth of organized crime networks, and deteriorating social conditions. The relationship between economic policies and political stability in Central Asia is not straightforward. However, the record suggests that a lack of economic opportunities can play a major role in fostering instability, particularly when it is compounded by perceptions of government mismanagement and political disenfranchisement. As the United States defines its policies toward the states of Central Asia, it must view economic development in the region as itself a long-term security concern. Popular discontent in Kyrgyzstan and Uzbekistan in early 2005 highlights the importance of these issues.

This report focuses on "fault lines" in the economic development of post-Soviet Central Asia and the implications for stability and the U.S. role in the region.[1] The analysis draws heavily from confidential interviews held with senior-level business executives and officials from nongovernmental organizations, government agencies, and international financial institutions within the United States from 2003–2005 and also during a research trip to Turkmenistan, Uzbekistan, Kazakhstan, and Russia in 2003, and the Persian Gulf in 2005. The core body of research has been updated since then. The research also includes a critical analysis of economic and social trends derived from official and unofficial statistics and reports. Chapter Two examines institutional and structural pathologies that have developed since independence, such as poverty, unemployment, corruption, and the shadow economy. Chapter Three reviews sectoral trends in agriculture, energy, and banking that will shape long-term economic growth. Chapter Four analyzes the effect of human development and social trends on economic growth and stability. Finally, Chapter Five offers concluding thoughts on the prospects for stability in the region, the role of foreign aid, and implications for U.S. policy.

---

[1] This structure is loosely borrowed from Wolf et al. (2003).

CHAPTER TWO

Economic Fault Lines

The states of post-Soviet Central Asia face unique institutional and structural challenges among the post-socialist transition states. Since the breakup of the Soviet Union, Central Asia has confronted significant transnational threats, particularly from the growth in drug trafficking, organized crime networks, and instability from Afghanistan, along with opportunities in the world market for its oil, natural gas, gold, and cotton exports. These have all played major roles in shaping the nature of governance in the region. Although poverty and the lack of economic opportunities are a part of the economic landscape throughout most of Central Asia, rising incomes, largely as a result of energy and other commodity exports, pose interesting and potentially highly divergent scenarios for development. This chapter attempts to analyze economic trends in Central Asia and draw implications for the prospects for economic reform and stability in the region.[1]

---

[1] According to Bohr (2004), the breakup of the Soviet Union led to the emergence of five new states in Central Asia that can only loosely be regarded as a regional entity by virtue of their geographic proximity. Characteristics such as low interregional trade intensity, high export trade dependence, and the prevalence of an informal economy imply a structural similarity to Africa more so than to Europe, North America, or Southeast Asia. Modern trade ties with industrialized markets in south and east Asia were inhibited by the lack of open seas and the inheritance of an energy and transportation infrastructure built to the needs of the Soviet Union.

3

Economic Overview

Following the collapse of the Soviet Union, most Central Asian states experienced a drop in economic output that far exceeded that of the U.S. Depression of the 1930s in both magnitude and duration, as illustrated in Figure 2.1.[2] Although the drastic declines seen in Tajikistan can largely be attributed to civil war, Turkmenistan, Kazakhstan, and Kyrgyzstan all suffered massive declines, partly as a result of losing long-standing internal markets and inter-Union

Figure 2.1
Comparison of Economic Recoveries in Central Asian Republics Compared with the U.S. Depression

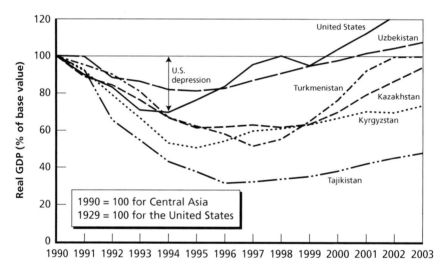

SOURCE: World Bank (2004).
RAND *MG417-2.1*

---

[2] Although the scale of the economic declines is worthy of note, a direct comparison with the U.S. Depression of the 1930s is difficult to make. For example, studies have shown that the size of the shadow economies of Central Asian states grew substantially during periods of economic decline in the 1990s. Thus, statistics on gross domestic product (GDP) could substantially underestimate total economic activity. Also, most residents of post-Soviet Central Asia owned their housing and enjoyed subsidies for energy and consumer goods, thus partly mitigating the effect of the economic downturn. GDP is also difficult to measure in the early years of independence. Nevertheless, the scale of the economic declines is large.

subsidies[3] within the former Soviet Union, exposing their uncompetitive industries to the global market. According to official statistics, Uzbekistan suffered the mildest economic setback among the states of Central Asia as a result of its concerted effort to delay political and economic reform.[4]

Official statistics show that the states of Central Asia, except for Kyrgyzstan and Tajikistan, experienced a steady recovery in economic output to 1990 levels. However, even if these statistics were accurate, they would be misleading. The decade of transition brought with it widespread poverty, unemployment, widening income inequality, the deterioration of social services, and the emergence of illegal drug use and associated epidemic diseases. Today, economic output in most of the Central Asian republics depends on a limited number of export commodities and external financing to support economic growth, and it has not provided sufficient job opportunities in the formal economy.[5] With the exception of Kazakhstan, Central Asian regimes today face significant constraints in their policymaking as a consequence of decisions made during the 1990s.

The difference in per capita economic output among the states of Central Asia is striking, as illustrated in Table 2.1. Although Kazakhstan's per capita income in 2004 was roughly similar to that of Turkey, Tajikistan had a per capita income similar to that of Mozambique.[6] Turkmenistan, which has recorded strong growth

---

[3] Direct subsidies from Moscow are estimated to have been as much as 20 percent of Uzbek GDP and 13 percent of Kyrgyz GDP. Indirect subsidies were measured to be 6.5 percent of GDP for Uzbekistan and 1.5 percent of GDP of Kyrgyzstan. See Rumer and Zhukov (2003, p. 64).

[4] Some have argued that in part this could be a statistical artifact resulting from overvaluation of the official economy (Taube and Zettelmeyer, 1998).

[5] Kazakhstan is the only country in Central Asia to have experienced a population decrease since independence (from 17 million in 1991 to less than 14.85 million in 2001), largely because of the emigration of Russians. But, population numbers have gradually been recovering as a result of rising birth rates and decreased emigration in recent years.

[6] Gross National Income (GNI) per capita (at Purchasing Power Parity—PPP). See World Bank (2004).

Table 2.1
Economic and Demographic Indicators in Central Asian Republics

	Kazakhstan	Kyrgyzstan	Tajikistan	Turkmenistan	Uzbekistan
Population (millions)	15	5	7	5	27
Population density (people/sq km)	6	26	45	10	61
Life expectancy at birth (years)	61.3	65.0	66.3	64.5	66.7
GDP (at PPP, $ billions, 2004)	112.1	9.8	7.7	34.6	48.5
GDP per capita (at PPP, $, 2004)	7,494	1,928	1,193	7,021	1,871
FDI ($ millions, cumulative 1991–2003)	16,873	461	223	917	1,314
FDI (% of GDP, 2003)	6.8	2.4	2.0	1.7	0.7
Income Inequality (Gini coefficient)[a]	0.32	0.29	0.33	0.45	0.35
Percentage below poverty line	21	73	74	34	47
Unemployment rate estimates					
CIA (2005)	8	18	40	60	28
EBRD (2003)	8.8	8.6	2.2	N.A.	0.3

SOURCES: Foreign direct investment (FDI) is from United Nations Conference on Trade and Development (2004) and World Bank (2005a). Life expectancy, GDP, and GDP per capita figures are from World Bank (2005a). Income inequality and poverty figures are from World Bank (2005b).The unemployment rate for Tajikistan is a 2002 estimate from Central Intelligence Agency (2005).
[a] The Gini Coefficient is a statistical measure of inequality, often used to measure income distribution. It ranges between zero (perfect equality) to one (perfect inequality).

rates in recent years, enjoys the highest per capita income in the region outside Kazakhstan. However, this statistic is very sensitive to fluctuations in natural gas revenues because of the country's relatively small population and large natural gas endowment. As shown in Table 2.1, in 2002, between 21 percent (Kazakhstan) and 74 percent (Tajikistan) of the population of Central Asia lived below the poverty line (defined as $2.15 per day (at PPP)).

After a difficult market transition period in the early 1990s, Kazakhstan has posted impressive economic growth figures in recent years, largely as a result of its relatively favorable geographic position, billions of dollars of foreign direct investment in its oil and gas sectors, and liberal economic policies (see Table 2.2). Kazakhstan has accounted for almost 50 percent of the region's total GDP and 85 percent of cumulative FDI since independence and is more closely

Table 2.2
Economic Growth Rates in Central Asian Republics (1991–2004)

Year	Kazakhstan	Kyrgyzstan	Tajikistan	Turkmenistan	Uzbekistan
1991	−11.0	−7.9	−7.1	−4.7	−0.5
1992	−5.3	−13.9	−29.0	−5.3	−11.2
1993	−9.2	−15.5	−16.4	−10.0	−2.3
1994	−12.6	−20.1	−21.3	−17.3	−5.2
1995	−8.2	−5.4	−12.4	−7.2	−0.9
1996	0.5	7.1	−16.7	−6.7	1.7
1997	1.7	9.9	1.7	−11.3	5.2
1998	−1.9	2.1	5.3	6.7	4.3
1999	2.7	3.7	3.7	16.5	4.3
2000	9.8	5.4	8.3	18.6	3.8
2001	13.5	5.3	10.2	20.4	4.2
2002	9.8	0.0	9.1	19.8	4.0
2003	9.3	7.0	10.2	16.9	4.2
2004	9.4	7.1	10.6	17.0	7.7

SOURCE: World Bank (2005a).

linked with Russia in terms of infrastructure and trade interdependence than with the rest of Central Asia. Both Kazakhstan and Russia are expected to join the World Trade Organization (WTO) in 2006.

Uzbekistan and Turkmenistan, both with substantial natural resources, have failed to implement any significant political and economic reform measures. Despite their economic potential, they have attracted the lowest FDI in the region, relative to the size of their economies, because of major state interventions in their economies and an unfavorable investment climate. Turkmenistan, a major natural gas producer, will likely remain an isolated, command economy, linked to the rest of the region primarily through natural gas trade. The prospects for Uzbekistan's long-term economic growth and stability remain uncertain and will depend on the regime's approach to balancing internal security challenges and political and economic liberalization.

Tajikistan and Kyrgyzstan, the smallest economies of the region, remain highly dependent on foreign assistance and an undiversified trade structure, which has made them highly sensitive to fluctuations in commodity prices (see Table 2.3). Kyrgyzstan's exports outside the Commonwealth of Independent States (CIS) consist primarily of gold extracted from the declining Kumtor gold mine. Although Kyrgyzstan has failed to attract FDI in other sectors of its economy, rising incomes in recent years have reduced poverty and increased demand for services. Russia has become an important export destination for Kyrgyzstan, particularly for electricity. Tajikistan's exports will continue to be dominated by aluminum, electricity, and cotton. Both Kyrgyzstan and Tajikistan suffer from a weak transportation infrastructure that has inhibited trade links both domestically and internationally. However, both have a relatively favorable track record with international donors, who are actively involved in infrastructure projects and debt restructuring, which will free up budget allocation for greater investment spending.

Table 2.3
Foreign Trade Commodity Structure in Central Asian Republics

Exports		Imports	
Kazakhstan, 2003			
Mineral and energy products	65.0	Machinery, equipment	43.0
Base metals	20.0	Chemicals	15.0
		Mineral products	12.0
Kyrgyzstan, 2002			
Precious and semiprecious metals	33.8	Mineral products	28.0
Mineral products	12.8	Machinery and equipment	15.2
Textiles	12.2	Chemicals	13.3
Uzbekistan, 2003			
Cotton	19.8	Machinery and equipment	44.4
Energy products	9.8	Plastics and plastic goods	12.8
Machinery and equipment	9.6	Foodstuffs	9.9
Turkmenistan, 2001			
Natural gas	57.0	Machinery and equipment	60.0
Crude and refined oil	26.0	Food products	15.0
Cotton fiber	3.0		
Tajikistan, 2001			
Aluminum	61.0	Alumina	24.7
Electricity	12.1	Electricity	12.2
Cotton fiber	10.9	Oil products	9.7

SOURCE: Economist Intelligence Unit (2005a, 2005b, 2005c, 2005d, and 2005e).
NOTE: Oil and gas export revenues are likely to be substantially higher for Central Asia in 2005 and 2006, on account of both increased export volumes and higher prices.

Poverty

Unemployment and underemployment are fundamental parts of the economic landscape of Central Asia today. The partial recovery in economic output during the 1990s was not accompanied by suffi-cient employment opportunities for the growing populations of

Central Asia. Despite a decreasing fertility rate, population growth in the region remains high and over next 30 years is estimated to average around 1.4 percent per year, the highest among the transition states.[7] Official unemployment figures, shown in Table 2.1, are notoriously unreliable,[8] with the possible exception of those of Kazakhstan, and do not fully reflect the fact that many of the nominally employed routinely experience wage arrears and are forced to hold multiple jobs to make a living. The percentage of working-age people in Uzbekistan who are employed declined by 12 percent from 1991 to 2002, despite the official recovery of economic output.[9] In Kazakhstan, however, strong economic growth has started to gradually reduce unemployment in recent years.

The main causes of poverty in the region were the massive output collapse in the 1990s, combined with changes in income distribution.[10] A sharp increase in income inequality throughout Central Asia particularly affected some subgroups, such as the rural populations, the less educated, and groups outside patronage networks. The states of Central Asia began the early 1990s with fairly equal distributions of income, with Gini coefficients ranging from 0.26 to 0.30.[11] The most unequal income distributions emerged in the relatively resource-rich economies of Kazakhstan, Turkmenistan, and Uzbekistan. However, Kazakhstan has a relatively more equitable income distribution than Uzbekistan and Turkmenistan in part because of its economic reform efforts.

Income inequality may have important short-term and long-term consequences in Central Asia. In many parts of the region, there is a deep perception that resources are squandered by deal-making among the ruling elite, at the expense of the average citizen.

---

[7] United Nations Population Fund (2005).

[8] In part, this reflects the fact that there is little incentive for the unemployed to register, since official unemployment assistance is scant throughout the region.

[9] World Bank (2003a).

[10] World Bank (2000).

[11] Inequality of consumption is less than inequality of income because of consumer subsidies and unregistered economic activity.

The perception of political and economic disenfranchisement may be a more powerful destabilizing factor than the absolute level of poverty itself. For example, the widening income gap in Kyrgyzstan between the more industrialized north and the impoverished south during President Akayev's tenure may have been an important contributor to the so-called "Tulip Revolution" in early 2005 (described in more detail in Chapter Five). In the long term, income inequality may also be an important determinant of future economic growth. Societies that have a larger proportion of people who cannot access loans, education, and insurance tend to suffer from underinvestment and thus lower long-term economic growth.[12]

The burdens of poverty have been exacerbated by the decline in public sector outlays for social services throughout Central Asia. In the early 1990s, all five governments of Central Asia subsidized enterprises facing imminent bankruptcy and consumers facing rising prices of goods and services, reducing public expenditures on health care and education. Consumer goods, wages, and pensions were seen as critical for social stability and welfare. In 2003, the Uzbek government began to significantly reduce public sector benefits, indicating possible strains on its budget.[13] In Tajikistan, substantial rises in utility tariffs were partly offset by targeted subsidies to low-income households.[14] In Turkmenistan, subsidies of utilities, fuel, consumer goods, wages, pensions, and student stipends are a corner-

---

[12] Deininger and Squire (1996, 1998); Aghion and Bolton, (1992); Alesina and Rodrik (1994); Birdsall, Ross, and Sabot (1995); Clarke (1995); Figini (1999).

[13] Although the government consistently authorizes nominal increases in payments to state sector employees, welfare recipients, and students, the true rate of inflation, which is probably twice the officially recorded rate of approximately 20 percent, will result in a significant drop in real income for these individuals. Also, to help finance its budget and also bring its energy and utility industries to world market levels as a precursor to privatization, the Uzbek government has steadily increased utility tariffs, which are currently below cost-recovery levels. See Economist Intelligence Unit (2003b, p. 23).

Even though many households own their apartments, the cost of services, such as water, electricity, and garbage collection, which used to be heavily subsidized by the government, can now be more expensive than a minimum state salary can afford. Interview with a business executive in Uzbekistan, May 2003.

[14] Economist Intelligence Unit (2003a).

stone of economic policy and are paid for through oil and gas revenues. However, the regularly scheduled doubling of wages for civil
servants—90 percent of the officially registered working population
is employed by the state—does not compensate for inflation and often results in wage arrears.[15]

Official economic statistics must be treated with caution in
Central Asia. The people of the area have shown a remarkable capacity to deal with unemployment and inadequate social provision
from the public sector by entering into the informal economy, culti-
vating subsistence plots, emigrating abroad, accessing latent social
networks, and, to a much lesser extent, receiving assistance from international organizations. Extended families and communities have
become the principal source of assistance to poor families. For example, the *mahalla*, a traditional Uzbek system of neighborhood
governance, has been a long-standing informal institution in Uzbekistan and within Uzbek communities outside Uzbekistan, particularly
in the Ferghana Valley. For centuries, mahallas have provided assistance to the poor in addition to performing other social functions.[16]
More recently, the government of Uzbekistan has enshrined the mahalla system within its legal structure by appointing the mahalla
leadership and channeling some government aid through this structure.

One major source of grievance in Central Asia has been the
chronic problem of unpaid wages, particularly in Uzbekistan[17] and

---

[15] Although the government no longer publishes inflation figures, inflation is probably
much higher than 8 percent, a figure published in 2000. Despite price controls, many
goods are purchased on the black market, eroding the real value of the Manat. See Economist Intelligence Unit (2003c).

[16] The mahalla can be a conservative institution that enforces standards of moral behavior
in a community. Mahallas are very diverse; some may well have been successful in providing
local economic relief, but others are alleged to be a vehicle for nepotism by the mahalla
leadership and even a source of intelligence for the government. The mahalla system has
received much attention as a tool for building civil society and as a means for targeting social assistance at the local level. However, it is still an open question whether a mahalla or
similar community structure is the most efficient and equitable way to target social assistance.

[17] World Bank (2003a).

Tajikistan,[18] which has resulted in similar poverty rates for both the employed and unemployed. During 2003, isolated incidents of labor strikes and protests occurred in different parts of Uzbekistan,[19] in part because of a liquidity crisis that exacerbated the wage arrears problem throughout the country.[20] The first cases of large-scale industrial unrest in Uzbekistan appeared during the summer of 2003, when workers at several major industrial sites conducted strikes after not being paid for many months.[21] In the past, Uzbek authorities have been able to localize such protests by targeting organizers, compensating workers, and deflecting responsibility.[22] However, the protests in Andijon during May 2005 and the subsequent crackdown by authorities may indicate that the government must choose between enacting fundamental economic reform measures or confronting internal threats to the regime with physical force.

Despite these problems, recent growth rates across Central Asia are a positive sign. For example, according to the International Monetary Fund (IMF), rising incomes and macroeconomic stability have helped reduce the incidence of poverty in Kyrgyzstan from 52

---

[18] A household survey in Tajikistan showed that more than 35 percent of the employed suffered from wage arrears.

[19] More than 100 pensioners protested in Urgench, angered at what they perceived as lavish regional government spending on hosting events and the drop in trade in the Khorezm region after the imposition of prohibitively large customs duties. In 2003, there were also protests in Andijan and Ferghana because of arrears in pensions and public-sector wages. See Institute for War and Peace Reporting (2003). According to a World Bank report, the pension system in Uzbekistan is not sustainable and will require further cuts in the future. See World Bank (2003c).

[20] During the summer of 2003, Uzbekistan began an unannounced austerity program to achieve exchange rate convertibility, leading to a liquidity crisis that has exacerbated the already widespread wage arrears problem.

[21] In July 2003, for example, wage arrears were the principal cause of a strike at a rubber plant in Angren, 100 kilometers southeast of Tashkent. See Institute for War and Peace Reporting (2003).

The first cases of large-scale industrial unrest may have been in August 2003, when workers at a refinery and petrochemical complex in Ferghana conducted strikes over wage arrears. See "Uzbek President Hammers Minister over Unpaid Wages" (2003).

[22] "Uzbek President Hammers Minister over Unpaid Wages" (2003).

percent in 2000 to 35 percent in 2004.[23] Yet, Kyrgyzstan was not immune to the political discontent that swept President Akayev out of office in early 2005. These events may indicate that the relationship between poverty and political stability in Central Asia is not straightforward and that perceptions of corruption and rising economic expectations may be critical in this regard.

The Shadow Economy

The shadow economy, which typically includes unregistered ("black"), partly registered ("gray"), and patently criminal economic activity, is an essential part of the total economic activity in Central Asia and will play an important role in the area's long-term economic development.[24] It is estimated that hundreds of millions of dollars worth of illegal or unregistered cash, most of it associated with narcotics trafficking and unreported remittances from migrant labor, is circulating in Central Asia.

During the 1990s, unregistered economic activity within the Central Asian republics created a buffering effect on total economic activity by growing during periods of recession and contracting during periods of growth.[25] However, the movements were not symmetrical, suggesting that it is more difficult to reverse the proliferation of unregulated economic activity and criminality than to bring them into being.[26] Since the shadow economy follows the market, an argument can be made that it serves as a necessary bridge toward economic diversification for transition economies that do not

---

[23] Economist Intelligence Unit (2005b).

[24] The black and gray economies are typically distinguished from patently criminal activities—criminal in their fundamental business model (such as drug smuggling), rather than criminal on account of avoiding regulations and taxes.

[25] Eilat and Zinnes (2000).

[26] Eilat and Zinnes found that when total economic activity (TEA) was falling, a dollar decrease in GDP was accompanied by a 31 percent increase in shadow activity, compared to a 25 percent decrease when TEA was rising.

have sufficient institutional capacity. However, it also distorts the competition that leads to growth, since much effort is spent on avoiding detection, and illegal enterprises must necessarily expect limited growth prospects if they do not enjoy tacit state protection. Furthermore, even if the shadow economy is more productive than the formal economy, it is not clear whether that is a result of attracting more clever businesspeople, favorable bureaucratic connections associated with unregistered business activity, or simply the avoidance of taxes and regulations.[27]

A sizable shadow economy is not unique to transition or developing economies. For instance, it has been estimated that Italy's shadow economy constitutes approximately 17 percent of its GDP. However, in major advanced economies, the shadow economy is rarely larger than 10 to 15 percent of total economic activity.[28] Estimates of Uzbekistan's shadow economy vary widely, but the most plausible estimates, according to the European Bank for Reconstruction and Development, are approximately equivalent to 30 percent of GDP.[29] Kazakhstan's shadow economy is estimated to be equivalent to about 25 to 33 percent of GDP.[30] Tajikistan likely has the largest shadow economy relative to the size of its economy in Central Asia, but estimates of its size are highly speculative because of the difficulties in estimating Tajik drug trafficking revenues and remittances from itinerant labor. In short, unregistered economic activity plays a major role in the economies of post-Soviet Central Asia.

Remittances from workers abroad are an increasingly important source of income for many households in Central Asia and also a crucial safety valve, especially in Tajikistan, where 500,000 to 1,500,000 have gone abroad to find work.[31] Most Tajik laborers work in Russia or Kazakhstan, where they can earn $200 to $400 per

---

[27] World Bank (2002).

[28] Williams (2003).

[29] European Bank for Reconstruction and Development (2003).

[30] "Kazakhstan Begins Process of Legalizing Shadow Economy" (2003).

[31] International Crisis Group (2003b).

month on some construction sites.[32] Remittances from legal migrant labor are part of the Central Asian shadow economy because the wages are almost never reported or taxed. Remittances from Tajiks working abroad have been estimated to be $40 million to $70 million per month, which would be equivalent to 40 to 75 percent of GDP.[33] It is estimated that there are more than 300,000 migrant workers in Russia from Kyrgyzstan (11.3 percent of Kyrgyzstan's working population), who provide remittances equivalent to 10 percent of Kyrgyz GDP.[34] Uzbek migrants to Russia and Kazakhstan are estimated to send home at least $500 million annually (approximately 5.7 percent of Uzbek GDP in 2003).[35] Although migrant labor has provided a vital source of income for some households in Central Asia, workers have been subjected to abuses on Russian and Kazakh farms and construction sites,[36] since they rarely have any legal standing. Also, income from migrant labor is usually barely sufficient to cover basic consumption items and is not a source for sustained economic growth.

As a result, there have been recent attempts to attract some of this income through capital amnesty programs and the reduction of customs duties. During the summer of 2003, a capital amnesty program in Tajikistan legalized $187 million worth of illegal currency—some of it from legitimate migrant labor and much of it from drug trafficking—by allowing Tajiks to legally deposit this money in one of eight major commercial banks without taxes or fines.[37] It is estimated that the population in Tajikistan is holding at least $500 million in unaccounted-for cash.[38] Kazakhstan was able to attract $480 million in a similar capital amnesty program in 2001

---

[32] International Crisis Group (2003b).

[33] Economist Intelligence Unit (2003a).

[34] Hill (2004).

[35] Hill (2004).

[36] Babakulov et al. (2003).

[37] Abdullayev (2003).

[38] Abdullayev (2003).

aimed at stemming capital flight that resulted from the turbulent tax and regulatory regime of the 1990s.[39] Kyrgyzstan has attempted to limit smuggling of goods into the country by reducing duties on legally imported gasoline, diesel, alcohol, medicine, and tobacco.[40] However, none of these measures alone are expected to make a significant dent in the shadow economies of Central Asia, if there are minimal prospects for gainful employment and entrepreneurship in the formal economy.

Corruption

Corruption is the use of public office for private gain and is generally characterized as involving private payments, pecuniary or in-kind, that undermine rules or substitute for the absence of them.[41] Economists often use the term "rent seeking" to characterize non-productive activities designed to generate personal wealth.[42] It is estimated that bribes cost private citizens at least $2.8 billion a year in the CIS.[43] Corruption may also prevent the type of cooperation needed between businesses and government to initiate a successful export-led growth of manufacturing as experienced in East Asia during the 1980s. Furthermore, corruption has had wider repercussions for the societies of Central Asia, because it has contributed to many citizens' feeling of alienation from their governments and has served as a recruiting tool for such groups as Hizb-ut-Tahrir.[44] Our focus in this discussion is on the effect of corruption on private investment resulting from the adjustments made by businesses and in-

---

[39] Zaslavski (2001).

[40] Goncharov (2003)

[41] Wolf et al. (2003).

[42] Williams (2003).

[43] Ledeneva (2003).

[44] Templer (2003).

dividuals rather than from the actual transfer of wealth between parties or any wider social effects.

The countries of Central Asia consistently fare very poorly in surveys of business perceptions of corruption. According to Transparency International (2004), all the countries in the region ranked in the bottom quartile of the 145 countries surveyed, as shown in Table 2.4. Although the Central Asian republics share similar corruption scores, a deeper look at the business environment in each country reveals substantial differences in the ways businesses operate, the types of corruption they face, and the implications for the international community.

Power and money in Central Asia tend to follow geographic as well as tribal or clan lines. These lines are quite complicated, with

Table 2.4
Perceptions of Corruption in Central Asian Republics (2004)

Country	Corruption Perceptions Index Score	World Ranking
Central Asia		
Kazakhstan	2.2	122
Kyrgyzstan	2.2	122
Tajikistan	2.0	133
Turkmenistan	2.0	133
Uzbekistan	2.3	114
Other		
Russia	2.8	90
Ukraine	2.2	122
Georgia	1.9	133
Azerbaijan	2.0	140

SOURCE: Transparency International (2004).
NOTES: The Corruption Perceptions Index score is a measure of business perceptions of corruption in a country as seen by business people and country analysts. It ranges from 0 (highly corrupt) to 10 (highly clean). The Transparency International study included 145 countries.

a range of competing ethnic, geographic, and religious loyalties claiming residents across borders. These clan structures can become critical power bases for presidents and legislators. At the local level, corruption is often a result of poor incentives.[45] Low wages and arrears have forced many citizens, including teachers, doctors, police officers, and others, to give preferential treatment in exchange for private payments. At the highest levels, rent seeking or corruption is often disguised as economic policy, where export revenues from hard-currency export commodities are used to subsidize other sectors of the economy through the discretionary use of exchange rates, off-budget accounts, and other mechanisms that allow for nontransparent financial transactions. Each state of Central Asia has employed some of the following nontransparent economic policies:

- Preferential access to favorable exchange rates through administrative "rationing" or discretion for special deals
- Off-budget accounts (i.e., slush funds) for hard currency exports, with access limited to a few
- Awards of monopolies or de facto monopolies through trade restrictions or creative joint venture structures.

The following analysis will focus on the experience of business executives in the three largest economies of Central Asia: Uzbekistan, Kazakhstan, and Turkmenistan.[46] Our focus is not the private gains per se but rather the deadweight losses to society, the misallocation of resources, and the chilling effect on private investment.

Kazakhstan

There is more corruption in Kazakhstan [than the rest of Central Asia], but they let you be successful here.

—Business executive in Central Asia

---

[45] Klitgaard and Baser (1997).

[46] Please refer to the Drug Trade and Human Trafficking section of Chapter Four for more information on corruption in Tajikistan.

Although the Kazakh financial sector is considered the most transparent in the region, Kazakhstan is also known by many investors for its "business-friendly" corruption. Some in the Kazakh business community have argued that corruption is simply the "untidiness of markets starting to work"[47] and has helped boost the economy by substituting bribes for time-consuming bureaucratic hurdles, thus creating a more efficient business environment.[48] Kazakh government officials are, on average, younger than most of their counterparts in the region, partly through the efforts of President Nazarbayev, who recruited a younger generation of technocrats, many of whom were trained in the West.[49]

Whether Kazakhstan's business-friendly corruption is of a truly different nature than the modus operandi within the rest of post-Soviet Central Asia is perhaps obscured by the fact that oil exploration and development and other highly profitable businesses have afforded investors in Kazakhstan substantial latitude in dealing with arbitrary lawsuits, fines, and other payments as a cost of doing business. One challenge for Kazakhstan will be attracting investment outside this sector.

Despite some notable successes in making revenues from the oil and gas sector more transparent through the establishment of the National Oil Fund, the Kazakh oil sector has recently been plagued by scandals that reach to the highest levels of the government. In March 2003, a U.S. investment banker was indicted on charges that he made more than $78 million in illegal payments through Swiss bank accounts to senior Kazakh officials, to win production-sharing agreements (PSAs) for western oil companies. However, it is highly unlikely that this case will have any effect on existing PSAs or the

---

[47] Interview with an economist in Uzbekistan, May–June 2003.

[48] Chebotarayov (2003).

[49] Interview with an economist in Central Asia, May 2003.

future involvement of major U.S. players in the development of the Kazakh oil and gas sectors.[50]

Despite setbacks in the investment climate, Kazakhstan is poised to become a second-tier energy producer in the next decade with little prospect that foreign multinational energy companies will shy away from its abundant resources. Recently, Kazakhstan has attempted to use its oil wealth to set up technology parks around the country to attract more foreign direct investment from engineering-based companies in nuclear research, biotechnology, and software.[51] This is part of Kazakhstan's broader strategy of diversifying its economy by actively promoting targeted industries to encourage technology transfer and lower the risks to private investors. However, this strategy risks encouraging corruption in the project allocation process because of the informal links between the business community and government officials.[52] It is unclear how the investment climate, born out of the highly lucrative oil industry, will accommodate this potential second wave of foreign investment.

Uzbekistan

In the early 1990s, there was one direction for the country, and it was honored at every level. Now, there are various centers of influence. It is hard to follow one line.

—Business executive in Uzbekistan

The nature of corruption in Uzbekistan may be a reflection of the power dynamic at the highest leadership positions, which has resulted in a lack of coherence as well as institutional ability within the country to implement national policy. According to many western business executives and government officials in the region, the oligarchic nature of the Uzbek regime is generally misunderstood by

---

[50] The Kazakh government hired public relations firms to repair its image in the wake of the scandal (often referred to as "Kazakhgate") and criticism over its human-rights record.

[51] Marsh (2003).

[52] Economist Intelligence Unit (2005a).

outsiders who view President Karimov as the principal impediment to political and economic reform. Rather, Uzbek economic policies are more likely the outcome of power struggles among the elite families within the regime, with Karimov serving in the role of "broker."[53] It is no surprise that government ministries are frequently at odds and that official statistics are typically unreliable, inaccessible, and decentralized, thereby retarding important economic decisions.[54]

During the early 1990s, Uzbekistan was considered to be a promising new market by many western investors who saw Tashkent as a hub in Central Asia, a potential market of 55 million people. However, with the collapse of gold and cotton prices, which had provided the Uzbek economy with almost two-thirds of its foreign exchange revenues, the Uzbek government introduced strict restrictions on foreign exchange conversions for trade and other operations in late 1996. By 1996–1997, businesses that had invested in Uzbekistan found themselves facing arbitrary prosecution, fines, and restrictions on currency conversion, as the "wheels fell off" the economy.[55] Many companies were forced to play on the black market and engage in joint venture agreements with state enterprises to survive.[56]

It is generally acknowledged in the diplomatic and business community in Uzbekistan that major policies in Uzbekistan are enacted to directly benefit high-level officials and their associates. These include trade restrictions, which grant high-level officials de facto monopoly control of commodity imports through creative joint venture agreements with shell companies.[57] However, a more significant concern to investors in the region is the lack of coherence in national policies and the multiple and conflicting sources of po-

---

[53] "U.S. Aid to Uzbekistan: Carrots and Sticks (Part 2)" (2004).

[54] Interview with a business executive in Uzbekistan, May 2003.

[55] Interview with a business executive in Uzbekistan, May 2003.

[56] "Uzbekistan is extremely ambivalent about foreign investment . . . they want cash but not foreign investors." Interview with a diplomat in Uzbekistan, May 2003.

[57] Interview with a foreign diplomat in Central Asia, May 2003.

litical and administrative influence in the country. Some business executives in the region describe the Uzbek business environment as one where "regime capitalism" and "private capitalism" compete, with the private sector essentially subsidizing the public sector.[58]

Thus, it is unlikely for entrepreneurs outside the traditional patronage networks to become independent political voices in Uzbekistan. According to investors in the region, a business in Uzbekistan, as a first condition, must not cross paths with any of the state or "royal family" interests, such as transport, communications, and media.[59] A small business must necessarily constrain its growth by "growing sideways" if it is to avoid the notice of local officials.[60] This phenomenon may have played a role in the arrest of 23 businessmen in Andijon and subsequent unrest in eastern Uzbekistan during May 2005.

Some western investors have been able to define a comfortable market niche for themselves in Uzbekistan. In fact, the high barrier to entry can provide some companies with substantial market power. However, lucrative opportunities are possible only for investors who are very experienced in the region.[61] The paradox for businesses of international scope is that although they have greater access to capital and political connections, they are also more heavily scrutinized not only by the local authorities but also by their own shareholders and, in some cases, public disclosure laws in their countries of origin.[62]

---

[58] Interview with a business executive in Central Asia, May 2003.

[59] Interview with a U.S. investor in Central Asia, May–June 2003.

[60] Interviews with a business executive in Uzbekistan and an economist in Central Asia, May–June 2003.

[61] Businesspeople who have found success in Uzbekistan often must employ the same tactics that are directed at them. For example, investors sometimes rely on former Soviet intelligence officers to investigate companies that they are interested in investing in or individuals they are considering for employment or business relationships, since official accounting records and academic degrees are considered highly suspect. Interviews with business executives in Central Asia, May–June 2003.

[62] "Generally, a large business keeps $100,000 to $200,000 aside for bribes here. However, bribery is not efficient, because society is fragmented. . . . Uzbek extortion usually does not

Corruption is a major source of grievance for both the average Uzbek citizen and for businesses that do not have high-level government facilitators. Western companies that have attempted to navigate the legal system in Uzbekistan have often found themselves inadvertently violating it.[63] The Uzbek court, with a history of near perfect conviction rates, generally does not provide satisfactory redress for companies that have been aggrieved or for individual defendants. Even when judges side with a defendant, the local hakim can unilaterally and without further review set the judgment aside.[64]

Many local and western business executives describe Uzbekistan as a "viable" or "real" country that is not living up to its economic potential because of incoherent national policy and the corrupt behavior of government officials, both of which make it impossible for businesses to achieve any sustainable growth. These conditions are likely to persist in a post-Karimov era unless significant reforms in public administration and governance are introduced, such as competitive recruitment and merit-based compensation in the civil service.

Turkmenistan

The only way for [businesses and donors] to operate in Turkmenistan is to be pragmatic and not oppose the government. Turkmenistan is at the crossroads of life. It is in a critical period. Turkmenistan needs good governance, but there is no capacity for this.

—*Diplomat in Turkmenistan*

According to many entrepreneurs in the region, business is exceptionally difficult for outsiders in Turkmenistan unless they are well-

---

involve Russian style mafia-violence, but they will make your business hell with red tape . . . it is impossible to legally make profits in Uzbekistan." Interview with a business executive in Uzbekistan, May 2003.

[63] Many small and medium-sized foreign businesses are members of the American Chamber of Commerce in Uzbekistan (AmCham), an organization that has helped foreign entrepreneurs maintain a unified voice on matters of economic regulation and adjudication affecting them.

[64] Interview with a business executive in Uzbekistan, May 2003.

connected at the highest levels of government. A fundamental problem for the business community is that officials in government ministries are frequently shuffled around in a "government merry-go-round," leading to a lack of competence and institutional memory within most ministries.[65] Some have argued that government targets for output, such as cotton, are purposely set unrealistically high to give President Niyazov a pretext to sack government officials at his whim.[66]

It is very difficult to get registered as a company in Turkmenistan, leaving some foreign investors, even those with government connections, in a legal limbo.[67] Many foreign companies operate under the aegis of inscrutable joint venture agreements with the government. A company's access to one of 20 or more unofficial exchange rates depends on deals reached with a specific ministry.[68] The Oil and Gas Ministry is known as the easiest government agency to work with, because it has the largest budget among the ministries and the authority for contracting and providing tenders. In fact, the Oil and Gas Ministry regularly finances projects that fall within the purview of other unrelated sectors, such as health and education.

Some have blamed western companies for starting a cycle of corruption, or at least bringing it to an unprecedented level, by enticing inexperienced government bureaucrats with lucrative contracts.[69] As a result, government ministers have been known to

---

[65] "You need to go to the deputy prime minister level to get stability in your government connections, since the shuffling happens a level below." Interview with a business executive in Turkmenistan, May 2003.

[66] Interview with an economist in Uzbekistan, May 2003.

[67] Interview with a business executive in Turkmenistan, May 2003.

[68] Interview with a diplomat in Uzbekistan, May 2003.

[69] "The developed world has no conscience . . . we corrupted [the Turkmenis]. The large technical contracts to supply equipment were designed around the size of the bribe and had nothing to do with the needs of the country." Interview with a diplomat in Turkmenistan, May 2003.

purchase large volumes of equipment that is dysfunctional or inappropriate for the specific needs of their industry.[70] Partly in response to such scandals, President Niyazov has been increasingly involved in all major contracts with foreign companies and has delayed privatizing onshore natural gas reserves, considered the crown jewel of Turkmenistan's natural resource base.

The inexperience of government officials and the growing isolationism of the country may have a major effect on economic development in the future, even into a post-Niyazov era. President Niyazov is a pivotal figure in all aspects of Turkmen society, involved in even seemingly minor economic decisions. For example, the exclusion of major foreign companies from the energy sector has meant that only niche energy players will be active in the oil and gas sector, diminishing the prospects for major upstream investment in the near term. Although Niyazov's decisions are dismissed by many outside Turkmenistan as misguided or even irrational, his gravitas brings some level of coherence to Turkmen economic policies. It is not clear what this lack of institutional capacity will entail for the international community and Turkmenistan in a post-Niyazov era, particularly for the development of the massive onshore natural gas fields, which will have a great effect on Turkmenistan's economic development. Turkmenistan's political and economic development remains perhaps the most unpredictable of all the post-Soviet Central Asian states.

Foreign Debt

External finance can stimulate economic growth by supporting faster rates of capital formation and smoothing consumption during economic cycles and commodity price fluctuations. However, the heavy external debt burden faced by several post-Soviet Central Asian countries poses a significant risk for long-term economic growth,

---

[70] Interview with a business executive in Turkmenistan.

particularly for the most indebted, such as Kyrgyzstan and Tajikistan, as illustrated in Table 2.5. From a situation of virtually zero debt in the early 1990s, debt dramatically increased during the last decade. The accumulation of external debt was primarily the consequence of chronic large trade deficits combined with a dramatic collapse of output in the early and mid-1990s.[71] Mistakes in trade and exchange rate policies, an inability to undertake fiscal adjustment, and foreign borrowing policies combined with already unfavorable external shocks (low commodity prices in the 1990s for major exports from Central Asian countries) were responsible for the debt buildup. As a consequence, all of the Central Asian states, excluding Kazakhstan, have a relatively high ratio of debt service to exports. This ratio is especially high for Turkmenistan and Uzbekistan despite their relatively low external debt ratios because they attracted primarily commercial external credits whereas other countries received concessional debt from international organizations, whose terms are typically less stringent.

Table 2.5
External Debt Indicators (2001)

Country	Debt as a % of:			Debt Service as a % of Exports
	GDP	Exports	Government Revenue[a]	
Kazakhstan	63	136	NA	12
Kyrgyzstan	128	336	550.4	24
Tajikistan	98	321	697.3	19
Turkmenistan	81	86	NA	31
Uzbekistan	75	165	111.2	30

SOURCE: European Bank for Reconstruction and Development (2002); Helbling et al. (2004).
[a] Net present value of external debt in 2000, as a percentage of government revenues.

---

[71] Helbling et al. (2004).

Most Central Asian countries are highly dependent on revenues from commodity exports. Commodity price fluctuations in world markets can severely affect external debt service ratios and therefore budget allocation. For example, the softening in world prices of cotton and gold (which account for almost two-thirds of Uzbekistan's export revenues) in the late 1990s negatively affected Uzbekistan's debt service ratio, leading in part to the fiscal strains seen over the past several years. The strengthening of oil, gas, cotton, and gold prices in recent years has improved this outlook. Nevertheless, in view of the fact that these countries started with a clean slate in 1991, since they did not inherit any debt from the former Soviet Union, these ratios indicate a rapid accumulation of external debt over a ten-year period of time.

The need to service relatively large amounts of external debt can discourage both domestic and foreign investment and adversely affect long-term economic growth. For example, 40 percent of projected fiscal revenues in Tajikistan are slated for debt repayment, leaving little room for social investment. In addition, a level of debt service exceeding 25 percent of export revenues is usually considered a threat to financial stability and can lead to popular disorder in extreme cases, as seen in Argentina in 2002. Significant bilateral debt can be an added concern when joined with an interdependent trade relationship. For example, Russia's acquisition of a significant portion of Armenia's power sector through debt-for-equity swaps has elicited concern about its overtures toward Tajikistan's strategic aluminum and hydroelectric facilities in debt-for-equity swaps.

CHAPTER THREE

Sectoral Trends and Implications

Agriculture

The agricultural sector accounts for a very large share of the workforce and is the employer of last resort in Central Asia. Since poverty is disproportionately severe in the countryside, agriculture will play a critical role in providing employment opportunities throughout the region, as shown in Table 3.1. Agricultural productivity and growth, however, are constrained by major state interventions in both input and output markets and by severe water shortages, particularly in the cotton and grain-growing areas in Uzbekistan and

Table 3.1
Rural Population and Agricultural Employment in Central Asian Republics

Country	Rural Population (%)	Agricultural Employment (%)	Irrigated Cropland (% of Agricultural Land in 1999)
Tajikistan	72	67	84
Kyrgyzstan	66	55	75
Uzbekistan	63	44	89
Turkmenistan	55	48	100
Kazakhstan	44	20	7

SOURCE: Micklin (2000).

Turkmenistan. Malnourishment has been a problem in some parts of Central Asia, particularly in Tajikistan and Kyrgyzstan.

Severe unemployment has led to a northerly seasonal migration from all the Central Asian states to Russia and Kazakhstan, as well as internal migration from rural to urban areas. Although the statistics on internal migration are scant, authorities have imposed and enhanced Soviet-era administrative and financial barriers to internal migration, particularly from the rural regions to the cities.[1] This has effectively segregated labor markets, particularly in Uzbekistan and Turkmenistan, leading to regional differentials in wages and unemployment rates.

Water and Irrigation

Approximately 70 percent of the land in Central Asia is agricultural land, of which only 14 percent is arable and the remainder under permanent pasture.[2] Agricultural land is dominated by the areas irrigated by the two large river systems—the Amu Darya and Syr Darya—whose headwaters begin in the glaciers and snowfields of the Pamir and Tian Shan mountain ranges, respectively, as shown in Figure 3.1. Approximately 22 million people depend directly or indirectly on this irrigation system in Central Asia. Although a native irrigation infrastructure existed for centuries in Central Asia, Soviet irrigation and distribution plans vastly increased the irrigated area in the Amu Darya and Syr Darya river basins from the 1950s to the 1980s. However, since the 1960s, over-irrigation of these rivers has led to the desiccation of the Aral Sea, resulting in significant ecological damage and desertification in the region.

The "upstream" and "downstream" states of Central Asia differ not only in their endowment of water and Soviet-era hydrological

---

[1] For example, young Uzbek men who travel to Tashkent to seek employment must pay exorbitant bribes to police to work within the city or face stiff fines if caught within the city limits. See International Crisis Group (2001).

[2] For a comprehensive review of irrigation and its historical evolution in Central Asia, see Micklin (2000).

Figure 3.1
Major Irrigation Regions in the Aral Sea Basin

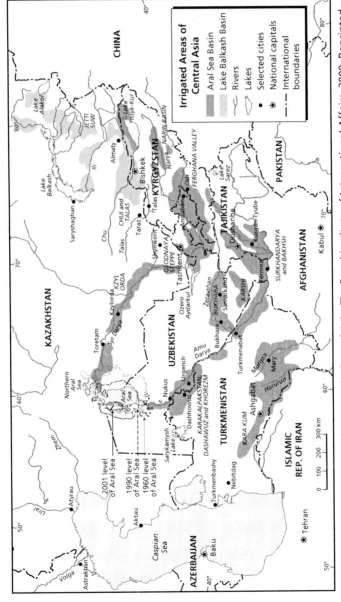

SOURCE: Philip Micklin, *Managing Water in Central Asia*, The Royal Institute of International Affairs, 2000. Reprinted with permission.

RAND *MG417-3.1*

infrastructure but also in their fossil-fuel resources. The lion's share of water is consumed by the fossil-fuel-rich downstream states of Uzbekistan, Turkmenistan, and Kazakhstan. As a result, water is a key security issue, particularly for Turkmenistan and Uzbekistan, which have a high demand for irrigation water to support agriculture. However, the hydrological infrastructure is controlled by the fossil-fuel-poor upstream states, Kyrgyzstan and Tajikistan. This has resulted in an interdependent trading relationship as shown in Figure 3.2. Although there is little prospect for a multilateral solution to water allocation in the region, the prospects for an interstate "water war" are very slim. Most conflicts have been local, with little or no ethnic dimension. Instead, inequitable water distribution has created social tensions and resentment of local officials who control water access within the agricultural sectors of virtually all the states of Central Asia.

Figure 3.2
Water Flows and Withdrawals in Central Asian Republics

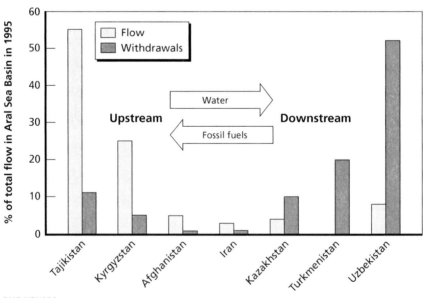

Although Central Asia has a long history of irrigated agriculture, there has been a problem of institutional competency in recent years, particularly in Turkmenistan, because of the high turnover of personnel in government offices and the highly politicized nature of agricultural targets and institutional reform.[3] Agricultural productivity has been disappointing in recent years in Uzbekistan and Turkmenistan, as a result of drought, mismanagement,[4] and lack of incentives for farmers.

Agriculture Policies

Since the collapse of the Soviet Union, the states of Central Asia have experienced different degrees of de-collectivization through their land and agricultural sector reform programs. Past experience has shown that such reforms are critical to the development of the agricultural sector, particularly when rural unemployment is a problem. China and Vietnam are examples of socialist countries that experienced rapid rural per capita income growth as a result of agricultural reforms. Land and agricultural sector reform have progressed the furthest in Kazakhstan and Kyrgyzstan; Turkmenistan and Uzbekistan have been the most conservative in promoting genuine reform.

Although agricultural privatization has achieved varied levels of success in the states of Central Asia, some common characteristics of small farmers throughout the region can be identified. Private farmers with modest plots are generally poor and have very limited access to credit. As a result, they have difficulty procuring basic production inputs, such as seeds, fertilizer, and equipment. In the states where collective farms have some de facto or de jure standing, private farms typically are still beholden to the goodwill of the collective leadership and local agricultural officials for water and other agricultural inputs.

---

[3] Furthermore, many Soviet-era agriculture specialists who were not of Turkmen descent have been removed from the agricultural sector. Interview with a diplomat in Central Asia, May–June 2003.

[4] According to western business executives in the region, agricultural officials in Uzbekistan and Turkmenistan frequently purchase equipment in the agricultural sector that poorly fits their needs and also malfunctions because of overuse and lack of maintenance and spare parts.

During periods of tight water supply, small private farmers are frequently denied water, whereas those who own plots near the point of withdrawal from the river (the upstream portion of the irrigation networks) are generally in a much more favorable position to secure steady water supplies. These coveted plots are typically claimed by former managers of the collective or other local officials. As a result, national policies are often ignored by local agricultural officials, leaving farmers discontented and frustrated.[5]

Kazakhstan has implemented the most progressive land reforms in Central Asia and is the least rural of Central Asian societies. However, the agricultural sector is still one of the largest employers in the country, and despite significant subsidies, is not a very profitable enterprise for farmers.[6] Reform measures in Kazakhstan aim to grow an independent, land-owning peasant class that can access the financial markets and procure insurance.[7] However, inefficient processing facilities and high production costs, which make Kazakhstan's agricultural products uncompetitive even in domestic markets, pose a concern for WTO accession in 2006.[8] Kazakhstan's main crop is wheat, which meets domestic demand and is an important export revenue source for the northwest and north central regions. Some economists have criticized Kazakhstan's development strategy for not properly addressing the problems of rural poverty and unemployment,[9] focusing instead on capital-intensive and high-tech industries.[10]

---

[5] Kholmuradov (2003).

[6] Economist Intelligence Unit (2005a).

[7] However, large farming interests hold sway over the Ministry of Agriculture. Interview with an economist in Central Asia, May–June 2003.

[8] Yermukanov (2004).

[9] At the same time, Kazakhstan is a very favorable destination for itinerant labor from other Central Asian republics, suggesting that rural Kazakhs' reservation wages could be quite high and that unemployment rates do not adequately reflect the employment opportunities in the region.

[10] According to one economist in Central Asia, "Kazakhstan is not asking for advice [from the international community] on basic and secondary education, but they want a value-added economy now, with dreams of a high-tech sector. . . . Every country wants high value-added. They feel they are rich in technology, but poor in labor. But if you have high unem-

Cotton is to Uzbekistan what oil is to Kazakhstan.

—*Economist in Central Asia*

Agricultural sector and land reform have been the least advanced in Uzbekistan and Turkmenistan. Although both governments provide subsidies to farmers, farmers must sell cotton and other commodities well below market prices, resulting in a net tax from the agricultural sector to the rest of the economy and the impoverishment of rural workers. Genuine reforms in the agricultural sector, such as liberalization of prices for wheat and cotton followed by long-term reforms in land distribution, would significantly increase rural incomes and potentially help stabilize rural unrest.[11] However, Uzbekistan maintains that it cannot reliably implement a transition strategy in the agricultural sector as Kazakhstan did, since more than 40 percent of government revenues come from cotton exports, and 70 percent of the population is employed in agriculture.[12] However, the sustainability of the cotton industry, often referred to as the "white gold" of Uzbekistan, is uncertain because of the deleterious effects of irrigation, including soil erosion, increased salinity, and contamination of drinking water. Nevertheless, both Turkmenistan and Uzbekistan are pursuing long-term plans to leverage their cotton production into value-added industries, such as cotton processing and textiles, which will likely be a target for state intervention in the future.[13]

---

ployment, you need to foster labor-intensive industries. . . . Nazarbayev knows that he must create jobs, but he's not focused on a development strategy that would do this."

[11] Olcott (2005).

[12] Cotton statistics, according to one specialist, are within 10 percent of their actual values in Uzbekistan, but Turkmen figures are generally regarded as largely unreliable by western analysts. Interview with an economist in Central Asia, May–June 2003.

[13] The Association of Light Industry in Uzbekistan plans to process one-third to one-half of all domestically grown cotton, since cotton yarn earns approximately double the price of cotton on the world market. Medium- and lower-quality cotton will be processed domestically, whereas the highest-value Uzbek cotton, particularly from the Bukhara region, will be exported. Turkmen state enterprises have entered into joint ventures with Turkish and European companies to build textile mills. However, the textile market is very competitive, and it remains to be seen whether native cotton will be processed into textiles within Uzbekistan and Turkmenistan. Interview with a cotton trader in Central Asia.

Kyrgyzstan and Tajikistan are the smallest states of Central Asia and also the two most rural and agrarian. Tajikistan grows only about 40 percent of its food needs and remains dependent on food aid and imports from abroad.[14] The lack of arable land and farm credit for crops other than cotton has discouraged private investment in such crops as fruits and vegetables in Tajikistan. Malnourishment will remain a challenge facing Tajikistan and Kyrgyzstan, both of which depend on international assistance, such as the European Union's (EU's) Food Security Program. Rural development in Tajikistan and Kyrgyzstan will depend, to a large degree, on progress in agricultural reform and on Uzbekistan opening up its borders to trade.

Energy

The Caspian Sea region promises to become an important supplier of non-OPEC oil to the world market and a major regional producer of natural gas over the next several decades. The potential opportunities from the energy sector present the states of Central Asia with three major challenges. First, they must provide the appropriate business climate to attract investment to build the necessary internal and transnational infrastructures to produce and deliver their energy products. Second, they must manage the future influx of resource wealth for long-term economic growth. Kazakhstan's and Turkmenistan's hydrocarbon exports are currently a critical source of government revenues, as shown in Table 3.2. Finally, the growth of the energy sector has increased the threat of militarization and terrorism in the region, posing a potential risk to Kazakhstan, Turkmenistan, and international energy investors.

Economic Effects

On balance, the existence of significant hydrocarbon and mineral reserves gives Kazakhstan and Turkmenistan, and to a lesser extent

---

[14] Economist Intelligence Unit (2003a).

Table 3.2
Central Asia Energy Reserves and Export Revenues

| State | Oil[a] | | Natural Gas[a] | | Oil and Gas Sales (% of Total Export Revenues) |
	Reserves (billion bbls)	Production (1,000 bbl/ day)	Reserves (Tcm)	Production (bcm)	
Central Asia					
Kazakhstan	39.6	1,295	3.00	18.5	58[b]
Turkmenistan	0.5	202	2.90	54.6	79[c]
Uzbekistan	0.6	152	1.86	55.8	10[d]
Other					
Azerbaijan	7.0	318	1.37	4.6	90[b]
Iran	132.5	4,081	27.50	85.5	80–90[e]
Iraq	115.0	2,027	3.17		>90[f]
Kuwait	99.0	2,424	1.57	9.7	95[b]
Qatar	15.2	990	25.78	39.2	85[b]
Russia	72.3	9,285	48.0	589.1	40
Saudi Arabia	262.7	10,584	6.75	64.0	90[b]
Venezuela	77.2	2,980	4.22	28.1	80[b]

SOURCES: [a] *BP Statistical Review of World Energy* (2005); [b] CIA (2005); [c] Asian Development Bank (2005); [d] CIA estimate (1998); [e] Energy Information Administration (2005a); [f] Energy Information Administration (2005b).
NOTE: Oil and gas export revenues are likely to be substantially higher for Central Asia in 2005 and 2006, on account of both increased export volumes and higher prices.

Uzbekistan and Kyrgyzstan, an opportunity to bolster their geopolitical relevance and economic development. Although they are only at the beginning of their post-Soviet hydrocarbon boom, Kazakhstan, Turkmenistan, and Uzbekistan already suffer from some of the classic institutional pathologies evident in other resource-rich regimes, such as oil and gas ministries that wield disproportionate influence over other elements of the government and off-budget petroleum (and other mineral) accounts. As shown in Table 3.2, Turkmenistan already resembles Persian Gulf states in its export profile, with Kazakhstan not far behind. Kazakhstan has made efforts to avoid some of the deleterious macroeconomic effects of increased hydrocarbon exports by establishing a national oil fund to shield its economy from volatile oil prices and exchange rate appreciation. The hydrocarbon sector will remain the principal source of economic expansion for Turkmenistan; gas revenues have allowed Turkmenistan to maintain widespread price controls and subsidies. Thus, securing natural gas export routes has been a top foreign policy priority for Turkmenistan.

Investment in the Energy Sector

The upstream energy (exploration and production) sector has been the major recipient of foreign direct investment in Central Asia, most of it in three oil and gas fields in Kazakhstan. Kazakhstan has invited major multinational energy companies to invest in exploration and production of its fossil-fuel reserves, but Turkmenistan has severely limited foreign company involvement, opening only its modest oil fields, which have not attracted much interest from multinational corporations. Uzbekistan's energy sector has recently received increasing attention from Russia and China. Russian President Vladimir Putin noted that Gazprom plans to invest $1 billion in the Uzbek economy. However, it is unlikely that Uzbekistan will be a major hydrocarbon exporter because of its large population and internal demand, but it may play a significant role in regional oil and gas transit.

The downstream (e.g., oil refining and distribution) and electric power sectors have suffered from underutilized capacity as a result of a loss of secure inputs from the Soviet era, collapsed demand, and a deterioration of infrastructure during the 1990s. Although Russia's RAO Unified Energy Systems (RAO-UES) has made overtures toward Central Asia's power sector, the prospects for profitability in this sector are poor in the near term and will require major investments and regulatory changes for long-term returns.[15] Fossil-fuel-poor Kyrgyzstan and Tajikistan have substantial hydroelectric power

---

[15] However, it should be noted that Kyrgyz exports of electricity to Russia exceeded 1 billion kilowatt-hours (kWh) in 2004. See RAO-UES Press Release (2004).

generation potential because of their favorable position near the headwaters of the great river systems in the region, but they are limited by poor markets and insufficient transmission infrastructure.[16]

Although Central Asian states have traditionally been reluctant to relinquish control of enterprises that they view as strategic national assets,[17] Russia is increasingly playing a major role in their energy sector. Since the end of the Russian financial crisis of 1998, both the Russian government and the Russian business elite have taken a more active interest in reestablishing business links with Central Asia, particularly in electricity transmission and hydrocarbon pipeline infrastructure. As a result, state-owned RAO-UES and Gazprom are often cited as instruments of Russian foreign policy in the region.[18] In fact, Central Asian natural gas is a vital part of Gazprom's current and medium-term strategy. Gazprom faces a choice of either investing billions of dollars in its own high-cost but promising Yamal Peninsula gas fields or relying on other sources of gas—Russian independents, oil companies, and Central Asian gas—which may eventually put pressure on its transportation monopoly.[19] Likewise, RAO-UES may view investments in Kyrgyz and Tajik water resources as more eco-

---

[16] The Tajik electric company, Barqi Tojik, has begun repairing transmission lines linking Tajikistan with Afghanistan and has started selling electricity to northern Afghanistan. Turkmenistan already sells electricity to the Herat province of Afghanistan and is expanding its transmission capacity. The Turkmen government signed an agreement with General Electric (GE) and Chalyk Energy in June 2003 to build new power plants and upgrade existing plants to increase electricity exports to Afghanistan.

[17] Turkmenistan, for example, has turned down an invitation from Chubais to join the CIS power system. "Turkmenistan Turns Down Invitation to Join CIS Power System" (2004).

[18] However, it is important to point out that RAO-UES is considered to be run in an impressively transparent manner in the region, and its relations with the Kremlin are not straightforward. Also, public opinion polls in Georgia indicate that Tbilisi residents feel that their service has improved dramatically since RAO-UES bought up most of the power grid in 2003, and the Georgian government has very positive relations with RAO-UES chief executive Anatoly Chubais and RAO-UES in spite of Georgia's ongoing tensions with Moscow.

[19] Personal communication with Katherine Hardin, Director of Caspian Energy, Cambridge Energy Research Associates, February 2006.

nomical alternatives to Siberian hydroelectric power.[20] However, it is unclear how current efforts to restructure the Russian electricity sector will affect RAO-UES and Russian investment in the region.

Despite scant prospects for profitability in the near future, RAO-UES has pursued a long-term strategy of a unified energy system in the Caucasus, controlling 80 percent of the Armenian power market through debt-for-equity swaps and a significant portion of the Georgian generation and distribution infrastructure. Chubais announced RAO-UES's plans for an "aggressive expansion"[21] throughout the region, with the Caucasus as an ideal "bridgehead" for RAO-UES's expansion into Turkey, particularly in underserved markets in the eastern part of the country.[22] In fact, RAO-UES has already synchronized the electric grids of all 14 of Russia's neighbors in preparation for a transcontinental grid. The EU and Russia had agreed to move toward a full integration of their grids by 2007 but many technical and regulatory questions remain.[23] According to Chubais, a vast east-west power grid from Vladivostok to Portugal could be created for as little as $100 million, which would be paid back within five years through cost savings realized from reducing power reserves and balancing peak requirements across different time zones.[24] However, recent electricity reform efforts in Russia have focused on attracting private capital flows into Russian domestic infrastructure and have slowed down acquisition activities outside Russia.

In recent years, the Russian-Chinese relationship, and the competition among Chinese, Russian, and even Indian companies, has

---

[20] Russia offered to reduce Tajikistan's substantial bilateral debt-service burden through debt-for-equity swaps of its Tursonzoda aluminum plant and hydroelectricity plants. Russia and Tajikistan have reached a preliminary agreement on writing off $50 million of Tajikistan's sovereign debt through equity in the Sangtuda hydropower plant. RAO-UES is already involved in projects in Kyrgyzstan and Tajikistan and has purchased generation assets in Kazakhstan.

[21] Startseva (2003a).

[22] Torbakov (2003).

[23] Startseva (2003b).

[24] Buchan (2002).

somewhat eclipsed the traditional centrality of the U.S.-Russian relationship in the region. Recently, energy security concerns have led Asian investors to show renewed interest in Central Asia's energy sector. Asian investors in Central Asia have enjoyed advantages over their Western and Russian competitors in the region, including a lower cost of capital, the packaging of larger cooperation agreements between governments, and a lack of competition among companies in international investments.[25] China has begun constructing an oil pipeline from Kazakhstan, primarily as a result of Russia's decision to shelve plans to build an oil pipeline from Siberia to China.[26] Analysts believe that almost 20 percent of Kazakhstan's oil production will be exported to East Asia by 2015.[27] China's demand for natural gas, which is expected to triple over the next decade, may eventually bring Kazakh gas to Chinese markets. However, the geographic position of Kazakhstan's gas, which is located primarily in its western region, may make a pipeline economically unattractive.

Export Options and International Relations

The political context surrounding the energy transit options in the region, often characterized in the past by a "lustrous compendium of conspiracy theories,"[28] may have settled down in recent years. Kazakhstan has largely succeeded in securing a diverse set of export options to match its desired production rates from its oil and gas

---

[25] Personal communication with Katherine Hardin, Director of Caspian Energy, Cambridge Energy Research Associates, February 2006.

[26] This project is a joint venture between China National Petroleum Corporation (CNPC) and KazMunaiGaz. The first phase of the project, a 988-kilometer oil pipeline from Atasu to Alanshankoy, on the Kazakh border, was completed on December 15, 2005, and is expected to make its first deliveries by mid-2006 with an initial capacity of 10 million tons (mt) per year. The second and third phases of this project will increase the pipeline capacity to 20 mt per year and eventually connect to Atyrau on the Caspian Sea. At the same time, China is constructing a 10–15 mt pipeline that will take oil from Alanshankoy to the Karamay refinery, which is owned by CNPC.

[27] Personal communication with Katherine Hardin, Director of Caspian Energy, Cambridge Energy Research Associates, February 2006.

[28] "Platts Guide to the Caspian" (2003).

reserves.[29] Turkmenistan, on the other hand, faces the dilemma of not having attractive nearby markets for its substantial natural gas resource base. Reluctant to commit itself to selling natural gas at below-market prices to Russia, which owns most of the pipeline infrastructure in the region, Turkmenistan entertained multiple export options during the 1990s, including westerly routes through the Caspian Sea and Azerbaijan, Iranian routes, and southerly routes through Afghanistan to the south Asian market.[30] However, the window of opportunity for Turkmenistan to diversify its export options by linking up with Azerbaijan via a trans-Caspian route has likely closed, and the prospects for a natural gas pipeline through Afghanistan, Pakistan, and India are slim because of security concerns and the uncertain political relationship between India and Pakistan.[31] Instead, in April 2003, Turkmenneftgaz signed a 25-year deal with Russian state-owned giant Gazprom, which will ensure it a steady stream of revenues and continued dependence on Russia.[32] This deal is consistent with President Putin's desire to reassert control of "dissipated" assets in Central Asia[33] and the vision of Russia and Central Asia as a "gas OPEC." However, the ever-changing relationship between Ukraine,

---

[29] However, recent delays in the expansion of the Caspian Pipeline Consortium (CPC) oil pipeline may constrain production growth, particularly as the giant Kashagan field begins to increase oil production over the next several years.

[30] For a review of the history and politics of Turkmenistan's natural gas export options, see Olcott (2004).

[31] Interviews with U.S. and Kazakh government officials. However, the Russian-Ukrainian gas dispute of January 2006 has renewed potential interest in the trans-Caspian pipeline to bypass Russia by linking Central Asian gas supplies with Turkey. Kazakhstan, whose support for the pipeline is critical, would also benefit by being able to leverage more generous export terms from Gazprom.

[32] Turkmenistan had originally set very soft terms for payments for gas, including payments in goods from Russia, Georgia, and Ukraine. In May 2003, Gazprom agreed to pay the equivalent of $44 US$ per thousand cubic meters ($1.32 US$ per MMBtu) from 2004 to 2007, one-half in cash and one-half in supplies of Russian equipment. From 2007 on, the price would be renegotiated at world prices. However, Turkmenistan has consistently demanded a higher price in recent years, and negotiations with Russia hinge on an audit of Turkmenistan gas reserves, in addition to larger geopolitical considerations regarding Russia's relationship with Ukraine and Europe.

[33] Olcott (2004).

Russia, and Turkmenistan on gas exports continues to change the investment dynamics in the region.

Although Turkmen gas production has grown steadily over the past several years, there is increasing skepticism concerning the state of Turkmenistan's natural gas reserves and the feasibility of its ambitious production targets. Although Turkmenistan has agreed to supply Gazprom with 80 Bcm of gas by 2010, it is likely that it will fall far short of this because of underinvestment in its gas sector, which is dominated by Turkmengaz. As a result, Gazprom has begun to hedge against possible production shortfalls from Turkmenistan by investing in Kazakhstan and Uzbekistan. Thus, over the long term, it is not entirely clear what role Turkmenistan's natural gas reserves will play in the region.

One potential solution to Turkmenistan's "stranded gas" problem is the large market in India.[34] As the world's sixth largest energy consumer with a rapidly growing economy, India's energy needs are driving its interest in Central Asia.[35] However, the necessary pipeline routes would have to traverse either Iran or Afghanistan, and then Pakistan, to reach India.[36] As a result, India is hesitant to depend on Turkmen gas, since Pakistan would be able to control the throughput. Iran and India have discussed the possibility of transporting liquefied natural gas (LNG) from Iran's South Pars gas field by tanker or of constructing a deepwater offshore gas pipeline to bypass Pakistan.[37] However, U.S. sanctions against Iran would preclude Ameri-

---

[34] However, energy analysts are increasingly skeptical of Turkmenistan's gas reserves and ability to supply gas for multiple export options.

[35] In particular, India's natural gas supply is not expected to meet its growth in electricity-generation-driven gas demand in the next decade. As a result, India has studied a wide range of options for securing its natural gas supply in the future, including overland pipelines from Central Asia, underwater pipelines from Iran, maritime shipments of liquefied natural gas, and alternative power plant fuels.

[36] A gas pipeline terminating in Pakistan is probably not an option, since Pakistan has enough gas reserves to satisfy its domestic consumption needs for approximately 18 years. Rather, Pakistan would benefit from transit fee revenues amounting to approximately $600 million per year, and an option to purchase the piped gas, if a pipeline were built with India as the final destination. See Vahidy and Fesharaki (2002).

[37] Hill and Spector (2001).

can participation and could constrain international involvement in the exploration of Iranian fields and the construction of appropriate infrastructure. Furthermore, both LNG and deepwater offshore pipelines would be very costly.

From October 1997 to December 4, 1998,[38] Unocal served as the development manager of the seven-member Central Asian Gas (CentGas) pipeline consortium, whose purpose was to evaluate and potentially participate in the construction of a gas pipeline from Turkmenistan to India via Afghanistan and Pakistan. The idea of the "CentGas" or "Trans-Afghan" pipeline (TAP) has been revived since the collapse of the Taliban regime, albeit with a different group of investors. The Asian Development Bank has sponsored feasibility studies to determine whether the massive onshore Dauletabad gasfields have sufficient reserves to justify the construction of a pipeline. Although the ADB announced in 2005 that the pipeline could be commercially viable, the final investment decision still depends on the participation of other credible investors.

Over the next several decades, the evolution of a global natural gas market poses interesting scenarios for the region. Many energy analysts estimate that approximately one-half of the natural gas reserves in the world are currently stranded.[39] However, with improving extraction and transportation technologies and increasing worldwide demand for natural gas,[40] it is expected that more unconventional or remote natural gas reserves will eventually be brought to market and that maritime transport as LNG may usher in a truly global natural gas market.[41] Russia (the "Saudi Arabia of natural gas"), Iran, and Qatar hold more than 50 percent of the world's

---

[38] Official Unocal statement concerning its withdrawal from the consortium, online at http://www.unocal.com/uclnews/98news/centgas.htm.

[39] Abundant gas reserves in many parts of the world are either flared or reinjected into oil wells to boost reservoir pressure rather than transported to markets, because of the high capital costs associated with natural gas pipeline construction and operation.

[40] The demand for natural gas is being driven primarily by its growing popularity as a fuel for electric power generation, such as high-efficiency combined-cycle plants.

[41] Yergin and Stoppard (2003).

natural gas reserves. Although the natural gas reserves in Central Asia are modest in absolute terms, the per capita endowment of sparsely populated Turkmenistan, for example, is the third highest in the world, after Qatar and Kuwait. Energy analysts envision the possibility of gas producers eventually exerting their market power and forming a cartel, akin to a "gas OPEC."[42] Although it is unlikely that Turkmenistan would become an LNG producer, since it is a landlocked country, it may play an increasingly important role in providing natural gas to Russia and Iran, both of which export significant quantities of gas to Europe and Turkey. Both would benefit from greater integration of the gas infrastructure assets with Turkmenistan, especially to serve their domestic markets.

Physical Risks to Energy Infrastructure

One effect of the reemergence of the Caspian shelf as a major oil and gas hub is the gradual militarization of the Caspian Sea area, as the littoral states continue to rationalize their post-Soviet military postures to protect their economic interests and border claims. However, a traditional interstate armed conflict without Russia's explicit or tacit approval would be highly unlikely, since Russia would be able to marshal overwhelming forces, if necessary, to preserve its interests. It is not clear how the U.S. military presence in the region will affect this relationship and whether any activities in the Caspian are categorically beyond the purview of the current U.S. security arrangement. The more likely effect of a military skirmish or legal stalemate on Caspian division would be to retard foreign direct investment in the region.[43]

A far greater risk associated with the dependence on oil and gas exports is the possibility of physical destruction of the means of production, storage, or delivery by nonstate actors. Kazakhstan and

---

[42] Yergin and Stoppard (2003).

[43] On July 23, 2001, Iranian gunboats threatened to use force against a BP research vessel operating in what Azerbaijan considers its territorial waters. This was followed by a declaration from Turkmenistan that Azerbaijan was illegally claiming oil fields in the Caspian Sea, since no demarcation line had yet been agreed on by the two nations.

Turkmenistan are clearly the most vulnerable to disruption, because their geographically dispersed and lightly guarded energy infrastructure offers soft targets to saboteurs. The nature of the potential threats, however, is less clear. Sabotage of this infrastructure, or extortion, could occur in many different ways,[44] affecting the revenue stream of both the government and multinational companies in the short run, particularly in Kazakhstan. For example, several major hydrocarbon gathering and processing facilities in western Kazakhstan are particularly vulnerable to sabotage from the air, land, and water. The effect of an attack on these installations would be much greater than that of an oil well fire or pipeline rupture, since they typically do not use "off-the-shelf" technologies, represent bottlenecks in the production process, and would require extensive environmental remediation. Kazakhstan is well aware of these vulnerabilities and has restructured its military districts and capabilities to deal with contingencies in the Caspian region.[45] However, it does not feel that it faces an imminent threat.[46] Furthermore, in the event of an emergency, the Kazakh Oil Fund would be able to insulate the budget from the revenue shock for some period of time.

In recent years, the vulnerability of oil and gas infrastructures has been highlighted by incidents of pipeline sabotage in Chechnya and Daghestan in Russia, Colombia, Nigeria, Iraq, and elsewhere.[47] Rebels and disenfranchised groups have disrupted pipeline operations in an attempt to deprive governments of petroleum revenues and, in

---

[44] Makarenko (2003).

[45] Interviews with government officials in Central Asia, May–June 2003.

[46] Interviews with government officials in Central Asia, May–June 2003.

[47] Oil and gas infrastructures are elaborate systems that include production, gathering, processing, transmission, storage, and distribution elements. Long-distance pipelines provide the most attractive and unprotected targets for saboteurs but also have the least effect on both the infrastructure itself and the surrounding community, depending on the location, timing, and magnitude of such an attack. For example, over the past decade, more than 750 attacks on oil pipelines have occurred in Columbia, mostly from the Caño Limón oil field complex in the Llanos basin to Coveñas. See "Nigeria, Colombia Pipeline Deaths Mounting" (1998). Rebels in Colombia bombed the overground Caño Limón-Coveñas oil pipeline 77 times in 1998 and more than 60 times in 1999, as a protest against the alleged involvement of foreign oil companies with right-wing paramilitary forces in Columbia. See Wade (2000).

some cases, to steal petroleum products. Although such incidents have generally failed to win major concessions from these regimes, they have increased the cost of petroleum operations and have drawn international attention to these regions. Such developments may pose serious concerns for the governments of Kazakhstan and Turkmenistan and for private investors in the region.[48] In particular, security concerns, in addition to the political and economic risk, have delayed serious pursuit of the so-called Trans-Afghan natural gas pipeline. However, it is highly unlikely that infrastructure sabotage could lead to catastrophic disruption of oil and gas operations in the region. For an act of infrastructure sabotage to have anything but a local and transient effect, it would have to involve extensive planning, resources, knowledge, and luck; and it would certainly need to be state-sponsored or at least to involve a dedicated group with significant financial means and trained personnel.

Banking

The development of the financial sector in Central Asia differs significantly across countries of the region. In general, banks are the dominant financial intermediaries in Central Asia. Nonbank financial institutions and stock markets are either at a very low level of development or nonexistent.[49] A growing and deepening divide has opened up between Kazakhstan and other countries in the banking sector, as shown by measures of monetary depth in Table 3.3. Kazakhstan has the most transparent and competitive banking sector and the most stable monetary system in the region. Although Kyrgyzstan has a relatively stable currency, its banking sector is

---

[48] Until mid-2002, Al Qaeda, under orders from Osama bin Laden, refrained from targeting petroleum infrastructure in the Gulf Region, regarding it as the heritage of the Arab nations. However, the planned attack on the Ras Tanura complex in Saudi Arabia in the summer of 2002 and the attack on the French-registered Limburg oil tanker in October 2002 represented a decided shift in Al Qaeda strategy. See Lia and Kjok (2004).

[49] De Nicoló (2003).

Table 3.3
Ratio of Money Supply to GDP

Country	1995	1998	1999	2000	2001	2002
Central Asia						
Kazakhstan	11.4	8.6	13.6	15.3	17.7	20.4
Kyrgyzstan	17.1	14.4	13.9	11.3	11.1	14.6
Tajikistan	19.1	8.1	6.8	8.3	7.9	6.0
Turkmenistan	18.4	10.4	9.0	11.8	NA	NA
Uzbekistan	17.7	15.4	13.6	NA	NA	NA
Other						
Russia	14.3	16.6	14.8	15.7	17.7	NA
Central and Eastern Europe and Baltic Republics	39.1	42.2	43.7	45.5	48.1	49.3

SOURCES: European Bank for Reconstruction and Development (2002); Asian Development Bank (2004); De Nicoló et al. (2003); authors' estimations.

significantly weaker than Kazakhstan's. Uzbekistan,[50] Turkmenistan, and Tajikistan have unstable or nonconvertible currencies along with uncompetitive and opaque banking sectors.

According to economists and business executives in the region, one key to regional development lies in Kazakhstan marshaling its considerable financial resources and expertise throughout Central Asia. This is already occurring in Kyrgyzstan, where Kazakh financial institutions have made significant inroads. However, Uzbekistan has a state-run banking system, where the five largest banks control most banking assets in the country.[51] Most banks in Turkmenistan and Uzbekistan engage in activities that are inappropriate for financial intermediaries, such as performing the functions of tax agents and

---

[50] Uzbekistan has accepted obligations of Article VIII of the IMF's Article of Agreements to eliminate restrictions on the payments and transfers for current international transactions. However, it has to go through serious economic and financial reforms to make its banking sector transparent and competitive. See IMF Press Release (2003).

[51] *Overview of SME Sector in the Republic of Uzbekistan* (2002).

statistical agencies in some cases. In particular, small and medium-sized enterprises (SMEs)[52] do not view banks as effective financial intermediaries in Uzbekistan because of restrictions on cash withdrawals, high interest rates, excessive documentation, and high collateral requirements.[53]

---

[52] Furthermore, since only about 1 percent of SMEs export products for hard currency, most SMEs in Uzbekistan do not access International Financial Institution (IFI) credit lines in Uzbek banks because of high exchange rate risk exposure.

[53] *Business Environment in Uzbekistan* (2002).

CHAPTER FOUR

Human Development and Social Trends

Health Care

Long-term economic development depends on a healthy, well-educated, and capable workforce. The deterioration of health care services in Central Asia has cast doubt on the region's ability to confront new health care challenges. In addition to the resurgence of infectious diseases[1] such as typhoid, and the contamination of the blood supply,[2] the incipient but rapid spread of HIV/AIDS from intravenous drug use is alarming.

Until 1991, the Semashko model of health organization—named after the first minister of health in Soviet Russia—featured total state authority and control; significant centralization of administration, planning, and financing; and free medical assistance at the point-of-delivery. Today, however, the remaining health care organizations suffer from a lack of resources. Health care providers receive

---

[1] International Crisis Group (2003c).

[2] See how states such as Kazakhstan are responding to crisis in *Strategic Program of Response to HIV/AIDS Epidemic within Ministry of Education and Science of the Republic of Kazakhstan for 2002–2005* (2002); *Program on Counteracting the AIDS Epidemic in the Republic of Kazakhstan for 2001–2005* (2001); *Program of Counteraction to HIV/AIDS Epidemic in the Armed Forces of the Republic of Kazakhstan for 2002–2005* (2002); and *On the Implementation of the Program on Counteracting the AIDS Epidemic in the Republic of Kazakhstan for 2001–2002: Material of the Meeting of Representatives of President of Kazakhstan Administration, Ministries, Agencies, and Local Executive Authority Bodies* (2001).

very low salaries, resulting in poor motivation and morale. Malpractice and substantial under-the-counter payments are widespread, causing public pessimism and distrust of hospitals, clinics, and pharmacies in both rural and urban settings.

Since independence, government expenditures for health care have declined for most of the post-Soviet Central Asian states, requiring significant private expenditures by citizens, as shown in Table 4.1. Officially, health care is free in all five Central Asian republics, as it was in the Soviet Union. However, health care has been de facto privatized in many parts of Central Asia, since private payments determine not only quality of care but access to it as well. Yet, there is virtually no provision for health insurance in most of Central Asia today, apart from some experimental reforms in Kazakhstan and Kyrgyzstan.

A World Bank survey found that two-thirds of health care users in Uzbekistan made unofficial payments, either in cash or in kind, directly to health care providers working in a public setting.[3] However, declining incomes have prevented most individuals from using private payments to make up for the lack of public provision of

Table 4.1
Public and Private Health Expenditures in Central Asian Republics

Country	Per Capita Expenditure, 2001 (PPP US$)	As a Percentage of GDP			
		Public, 2001	Private, 2001	Total, 2001	Total, 1990
Kazakhstan	204	1.9	1.2	3.1	3.2
Kyrgyzstan	108	1.9	2.1	4.0	4.7
Tajikistan	43	1.0	2.3	3.3	4.9
Turkmenistan	245	3.0	1.1	4.1	4.0
Uzbekistan	91	2.7	0.9	3.6	4.6

SOURCES: United Nations Development Programme (2003, 2004).

---

[3] World Bank (2003c).

health care. The survey found that such payments were a significant burden on the poor and that the costs of chronic or catastrophic care could relegate the nonpoor to poverty. As a result, most households cannot afford to seek primary health care, resulting in the aggravation of treatable conditions.

Health care reform has proceeded very slowly because of the Soviet legacy of hierarchical health administration. However, tighter budgets and pressure from international financial institutions to make social spending more efficient are forcing the reassessment of health care delivery methods. Acknowledging the collapse of its health care system, the parliament of Tajikistan has recommended amending the constitution to abolish the system of nominally free health care and, in turn, has set fixed prices for medical coverage to reduce the bribery.[4] In Kyrgyzstan, a copayment medical insurance policy was introduced in two regions in March 2001, resulting in reduced informal payments to medical staff and for medical supplies.[5] In February 2005, President Niyazov decreed that all regional and district hospitals in Turkmenistan be closed and replaced by diagnostic centers. Although this policy has been promoted as a step toward modernizing the health care sector, it is likely a cost-cutting measure that will reduce access to care for patients outside Ashgabat.[6] The international financial institutions and nongovernmental organizations have urged Kazakhstan to increase its health care budget because of its favorable fiscal position.[7] Recent growth rates across Central Asia may result in greater health care investment in the future, which could help address some of the problems.

A deteriorating health care sector may affect the region in several ways, the most likely of which is an inability to handle a growing HIV/AIDS epidemic, which could harm long-term economic growth. Emergency response and health care services in the region are also ill-

---

[4] Najibullah (2003).

[5] Tracy (2003).

[6] Economist Intelligence Unit (2005c).

[7] Interviews with nongovernmental organizations and economists in Central Asia.

equipped to handle major natural disasters[8] or refugee situations. Such events would put pressure on the governments in the region to allow large-scale foreign assistance and parallel health care structures operated outside direct government control. It is interesting to note that, in the aftermath of the Kashmir earthquakes of 2005, the best organized aid groups were often led by religious parties rather than government agencies.[9]

Education

One great legacy that Central Asia inherited from the Soviet Union was its rigorous educational system and emphasis on technical training. Although Central Asia still enjoys a high level of literacy for its level of income, the steady deterioration of the educational system over the past decade has increased the mismatch between the skill set of young Central Asians and that demanded by the global market, potentially retarding long-term economic growth.[10] Public expenditures on education have declined, particularly in Kyrgyzstan and Tajikistan, whereas reliable figures for Turkmenistan are not available.[11]

However, an even greater concern may be the change in the nature of educational instruction and the lack of motivation for students to complete educational degrees, especially when returns in the job market are highly uncertain. In many cases, children of the poor, particularly in rural regions of Central Asia, are taken out of school early to work. The International Organization for Migration (IOM) estimates that children harvest 40 percent of Tajikistan's cotton dur-

---

[8] For example, Central Asia has a history of seismic activity, resulting in major earthquakes in Ashgabat, Turkmenistan (1948), Tashkent, Uzbekistan (1886 and 1966), Almaty, Kazakhstan (1887 and 1910), and Dushanbe, Tajikistan (1907).

[9] Baldauf and Winter (2005).

[10] World Bank (2003b).

[11] United Nations Development Programme (2002, 2003).

ing the four- to five-month season, adversely affecting their education and health.[12]

The situation is particularly dire in Turkmenistan, where educational standards have deteriorated significantly in recent years. Although the Soviet educational system always included an important ideological component, its technical training competed with, and in some cases may have exceeded, that of the developed world. However, the Turkmen educational system, under the direction of President Niyazov, has reorganized its curriculum to focus almost solely on Turkmen history and culture, as interpreted through Niyazov's autobiography, the *Rukhnama* ("Book of the Soul"), which is presented as a comprehensive spiritual and educational guide for the Turkmen people. Russian language training has been jettisoned to a greater degree than in the rest of Central Asia, thus depriving students of learning what is still the lingua franca of the region. This erosion of education will continue in the future unless significant measures are taken to countermand these dropping educational standards. The effects of these policies are already evident today. Companies involved in telecommunications, information technology, or engineering-based industries typically do not recruit young graduates from Turkmen universities but rather turn to older, Soviet-trained engineers or foreign experts, because of the dearth of highly qualified skilled labor among the newer graduates.[13]

Many observers credit the Uzbek leadership, on the other hand, with maintaining an emphasis on education despite the economic uncertainties of the past decade. Uzbekistan maintained the highest regional spending on education, as a percentage of GDP, during the 1990s. However, the dearth of job opportunities has reduced the motivation for many young Uzbeks to pursue a higher education. Furthermore, the status of teachers has diminished significantly.[14] West-

---

[12] "Report Says Children Harvest 40 Percent of Tajik Cotton" (2004).

[13] Interviews with business executives in Turkmenistan.

[14] For example, in Uzbekistan, school administrators and teachers once received salaries commensurate with government ministers and officials but now hold multiple jobs to make

ern business executives are increasingly distrustful of the academic credentials of university graduates because of the erosion of academic standards and allegations of bribery for grades within the educational system.[15] Unfortunately, attempts to provide western-style business school curricula and testing have been met with labyrinthine government restrictions in Uzbekistan.[16] Business executives note that there is consistently a greater demand than supply of recent graduates with such training.

The steady deterioration of the educational standards in Central Asia has eroded the region's attractiveness as a potential source of high-skilled, low-cost labor to foreign investors. The upswing in economic growth in recent years may lead to increasing expenditures on public education. However, budget allocation for education is not the only issue. Thus far, there is little evidence that the countries of Central Asia have made the decisions to either update their curricula to meet the demands of the global economy or encourage students to study abroad, as some other nations in Asia have done to their benefit.

Finally, the question remains whether youth in Central Asia have responded to deteriorating incentives for public education by increasingly seeking other educational or developmental opportunities outside the purview of the government. Decreasing attendance rates throughout the region may simply indicate that a larger proportion of students are entering the workforce early, particularly in agriculture. However, it may also suggest that other influences, such as political Islam and organized crime, could be playing an increasingly active role in shaping the experiences of the young generation of Central Asia.

---

a living and no longer benefit from a 50 percent discount on housing and utilities. See Economist Intelligence Unit (2003b); interview with an official in Uzbekistan.

[15] Interviews with business executives in Uzbekistan.

[16] Interviews with officials in Central Asia.

Drug Trade and Human Trafficking

The narcotics trade and human trafficking will have lasting effects on Central Asia, not only for their destructive impact on the health and welfare of the population but also because they have attracted organized crime in the region.

Drug Trade

The prognosis in terms of drugs and crime is not optimistic. All Central Asian governments, to a greater or lesser extent, deny the fact that organized narcotics traffickers are active within their territories, preferring to regard the phenomenon as an external issue. Four of six main drugs routes from Afghanistan to western markets pass through the Central Asian republics (three through Tajikistan, one through Turkmenistan).

Criminal organizations exporting Afghan narcotics were compelled to find alternative routes as a result of Iran's recent successes in interdicting Afghanistan heroin traffic. Heroin repositories and laboratories are located in the Pamir mountains in Afghanistan, near the border of Tajikistan. Chemical precursors flow in the opposite direction, from the CIS, Iran, and Pakistan to Afghanistan. In fact, the same rail and surface routes that annually transport thousands of tons of legal products, such as cotton, are increasingly used by drug traffickers.[17] Traffickers can allegedly smuggle heroin by inserting it within the dense cotton bales, which make it difficult for dogs to detect, and sophisticated narcotics detection equipment is often not used properly by the border guards in the region.[18]

Narcotics are increasingly being trafficked as refined heroin rather than opium because it is easier to transport and more profitable. This trade is well organized and lucrative. According to General Andrey Nikolaev, former Director of the Russian Federal Border Service (FPS), a kilogram of heroin costs $100 in Badakhshan Prov-

---

[17] Interview with a diplomat in Uzbekistan, May 2003.

[18] Interviews in Central Asia, May–June 2003.

ince in Afghanistan. Once it is smuggled across the River Panj into the Gorno-Badakhshan Autonomous Region in Tajikistan, its value increases to $1,000. As it is taken through Osh in Kyrgyzstan, it increases to $10,000; when it reaches Europe it costs $100,000.[19] Thus, the return from massive and illicit opium cultivation in Afghanistan in 2002—totalling more than 3,400 tons, or around three-quarters of the world's total—has turned Central Asia into a center for international heroin trafficking. This is shown by increasing seizures of multiton shipments of opiates in the region. Countries like Tajikistan, Uzbekistan, and Kyrgyzstan are seeing more trafficking of processed heroin, higher levels of heroin purity, and more vigilant, aggressive, and better organized trafficking operations, in particular since opium production has moved into the northern provinces of Afghanistan—a region with close and direct routes into Central Asia.[20]

Turkmenistan is the only country in post-Soviet Central Asia that has shown a steady decrease in heroin seizures since 1997.[21] In fact, seizures in Turkmenistan have dropped sharply, and it is not clear whether this reflects reduced traffic flows through Turkmenistan, less-effective interdiction, or the collusion of elements of the regime with organized crime.[22] Publicly available data are not particularly helpful in this regard, which illustrates the inscrutable nature of the drug trade, organized crime, and governance in Central Asia today. The International Narcotics Control Board has singled out Turkmenistan for its lack of cooperation in the international community's efforts to curb narcotics trafficking. In particular, Turkmenistan does not participate in Operation Topaz, which monitors the traffic of acetic anhydride—a critical component in the manufacture of heroin, which is possibly being smuggled from Turkmenistan to Afghanistan.[23]

---

[19] See Ruban (2001).

[20] United Nations Information Service (2003).

[21] United Nations Office of Drug and Crime (2003).

[22] Interviews in Turkmenistan, May–June 2003; International Crisis Group (2003c).

[23] ". . . And Criticizes Turkmenistan's Lack of Cooperation" (2004).

Drug trafficking may be a significant source of income for some Central Asian economies. Gross drug trafficking profits within Central Asia are estimated to have been equivalent to 7 percent of the region's aggregate GDP in 2001 and much higher for Tajikistan, according to the United Nations Office of Drug and Crime.[24] However, it is difficult to measure the actual revenues and income accruing to Central Asian traffickers. Gross margins can be estimated with reasonable accuracy by surveying the market price of narcotics at the origin (e.g., the Afghan border) and final destination (e.g., Russia). However, net margins, which represent the actual revenues to the traffickers, are much less reliable and seldom estimated, since they must reflect the bribes paid to border guards, various state authorities, and narco-mafia distribution channels. Capital amnesty programs, such as a recent one in Tajikistan, may give some indication of the magnitude of illegal cash in the Tajik economy, which is on the order of hundreds of millions of dollars. By comparison, the GDP (at market exchange rates) of Tajikistan in 2002 was estimated to be approximately $1.2 billion, which suggests that illegal drugs are a significant part of the Tajik economy.[25] However, it is estimated that income from illicit drug trafficking contributes significantly less to local economic development than the equivalent income from legal products, since a substantial portion of drug revenues are invested abroad or used to purchase imported, luxury goods, reducing the beneficial multiplier effect on an economy.[26]

The drug trade fosters other problems, as the rate of usage rises in the countries that serve as transit routes for traditional markets. Of particular concern is the number of HIV/AIDS and hepatitis A/B/C infections, which have increased in Central Asia at least in part because the rate of intravenous injection of opiates is soaring. This follows patterns observed in Russia, Ukraine, and elsewhere where HIV

---

[24] United Nations Office of Drug and Crime (2003).

[25] Economist Intelligence Unit (2003a).

[26] The International Narcotics Control Board (INBC) estimates that illicit drug trafficking contributed 36 percent less to local economic development than equivalent income from legal products. "Report of the International Narcotics Board Control" (2002, p. 3).

infections first emerged as a problem among intravenous drug users, subsequently spreading much more widely as a sexually transmitted disease. There are fears that the numbers of infections may further multiply as heroin is widely and easily available.[27] Many share their injecting equipment, and blood is used to prepare the drugs, in spite of the risk of HIV/AIDS. Many users know nothing about HIV/AIDS and how to prevent it. A rapid situation assessment found that 30 percent of commercial sex workers are estimated to be using illicit drugs.[28]

Human Trafficking

Official statistics on human trafficking in Central Asia are scant. IOM estimates that 4,000 women from Kyrgyzstan, 5,000 from Kazakhstan, and 1,000 from Tajikistan are trafficked every year.[29] There is evidence that some victims, primarily young women, are trafficked for commercial sexual exploitation by Central Asian and Russian organized crime networks operating out of Southeast Asia and the Persian Gulf.[30] There are also reports of human "markets" in Kazakhstan and Uzbekistan for destinations in the Persian Gulf and Europe.[31] However, trafficking in persons is not limited to the sex industry. From Central Asia, illegal service sector labor has become a lucrative criminal market for basic industries throughout Eurasia and the Persian Gulf region, including the United Arab Emirates, Israel, Iran, Thailand, South Korea, Russia, and Germany. But there is also trafficking among the five republics.

Recently, Tajikistan and Kazakhstan amended articles in their criminal codes to make it easier to prosecute traffickers. There have also been recent efforts by the Uzbek government, with help from the

---

[27] United Nations Information Service (2003).

[28] Peak (2001).

[29] International Organization on Migration website, online at http://www.iom.int. Also, Sulaimanova (2004).

[30] Orhant (2003).

[31] Interviews in Turkmenistan, Uzbekistan, and Kazakhstan, May–June 2003.

U.S. Agency for International Development (USAID), to take preventive measures.[32] However, local law enforcement agencies find it difficult to eliminate human trafficking because it involves highly organized and well-connected criminal syndicates capable of bribing border police and other officials.[33] In some cases, the criminals obtain fake passports for the victims to hide their ages, make the travel arrangements, and obtain visas on business grounds under the guise of shopping trips.[34] Unfortunately, a large volume of trafficking is voluntary. Until recently, the governments in Central Asia preferred to ignore the issue. Victims often do not report their experiences to the police in the countries they have been trafficked to, since they do not speak the local language, have little or no knowledge of the area, and have no legal status. In most cases, the traffickers take the victim's passport. Some of the victims eventually are detained by police and deported to their home countries; other simply disappear.[35]

Trafficking and Organized Crime

Organized crime in Central Asia is a significant contributor to the drug trade and human trafficking. Many criminal networks in the Central Asian states are tied directly to people who either work for the government or are affiliated with businesses such as freight companies.[36] In addition, major human smuggling networks operate within Central Asia with the explicit knowledge of local authorities, luring victims to work in Europe and the Middle East by using increasingly sophisticated schemes to circumvent any type of legal recourse.[37] It is not known whether drug money is linked to insurgent groups in the region, since such allegations are based primarily on

---

[32] "Government Takes Steps to Prevent Human Trafficking" (2003).

[33] Interview with an investor in Central Asia, March 2003.

[34] "Lure of the West" (2001).

[35] However, victims are often reluctant to return home for fear of ostracism, particularly in more conservative rural communities in Central Asia.

[36] Interview with the International Crisis Group, April 2005.

[37] Interviews in the United Arab Emirates, April 2005.

anecdotal information. Until the Central Asian governments seek accountability of their own state employees and companies that operate in their territory, drug and human trafficking will continue, since collaboration to fight such activity is not in the interests of those who benefit financially from illegal trade.

CHAPTER FIVE

Conclusions and Implications for the United States

Prospects for Development in the Region

Recent events call to attention the long-term economic and social trends in Central Asia and their effect on stability and broader U.S. interests in the region. This chapter aims to integrate the discussion from previous chapters and draw policy conclusions in light of these events. Economic problems served as crucial focal points for popular discontent in both Kyrgyzstan and Uzbekistan in 2005. However, regional experts provide strikingly diverse assessments on the prospects for economic development and stability in Central Asia, potentially resulting in equally divergent implications for U.S. policies. As events unfold, such assessments will evolve, but several possible outcomes are worthy of note.

As discussed in Chapter Two, corruption has not only had a deleterious effect on economic development in Central Asia, but it may also be an important contributor to political instability. The so-called "Tulip Revolution" in Kyrgyzstan in early 2005 was driven, in part, by the perception among southern elites that former President Akayev's patronage networks were resulting in their economic disenfranchisement and a widening income gap between the north and the south.[1] President Bakiev, who gained his anticorruption credentials during his tenure as the former prime minister of Kyrgyzstan, has identified the elimination of corruption as one of his main goals in office.[2] Although the long-term repercussions of the Kyrgyz events are not yet clear, at a minimum they represent an attempted redistribution of power and wealth among the competing clans that have vied for power since 1991. As a small nation heavily reliant on foreign assistance, Kyrgyzstan has continued to pursue good relations with its external patrons after Akayev's fall, hosting both the U.S. and Russian military presence and reaffirming its commitments with the IMF.[3] Under pressure from partners in the Shanghai Cooperation Organization, Bakiev initially raised the issue of the U.S. base in Manas, but since agreed to long-term basing rights until the situation in Afghanistan is "completely stabilized."[4]

Agriculture, land reform, and trade policies have also taken center stage with the unrest in Uzbekistan in 2004 and 2005. Since late 2004, the Ferghana Valley and neighboring regions of eastern Uzbekistan have been the site of protests against restrictive state policies on commerce. The events leading to the crackdown on protestors in Andijon may have been an expression of the rising expectations of the population, as demonstrated by the emergence of a small group of businessmen seeking their own solutions to the economic situation in the Ferghana Valley.[5] Economic reform in the agricultural sector may

---

[1] During President Akayev's tenure, Kyrgyzstan experienced a widening income gap between the south and the more industrialized north. The two regions had effectively functioned as separate entities, on account of poor north-south infrastructural linkages and long-standing patronage networks that determined the allocation of resources within the country.

[2] Since Akayev's ouster, a number of prominent individuals have been under investigation for bribing the former president, including an illegal transfer of $480 million by the head of the National Bank to the presidential account. Marat (2005).

[3] Economist Intelligence Unit (2005b).

[4] It is estimated that the net impact of base-related activities and transfers amounted to approximately 5 percent of Kyrgyzstan's GDP in 2004. Cooley (2005). One impediment to this agreement has been Kyrgyzstan demanding an accounting of previous payments, which were alleged to have been stolen by fuel supply companies closely allied with the previous Akayev regime. Sevastopulo and Wetzel (2005); Brinkley (2005).

[5] Schwartz (2005).

have a direct effect on stability in Uzbekistan, as discussed in Chapter Three. In particular, President Karimov may be able to stabilize the situation by liberalizing prices for wheat and cotton—which would significantly increase rural incomes—and commencing long-term reforms in land distribution, trade regulations, and the judicial system.[6]

The political transitions in Georgia, Ukraine, and Kyrgyzstan have served notice to the regimes in the region, which have steadily delayed economic reform and increased pressure on political opposition groups and nongovernmental organizations, to different degrees. The government of Kazakhstan has attempted to prevent political opposition from becoming a cohesive force by limiting the scope of political activity in the country and co-opting opposition leadership.[7] President Rahmonov has publicly criticized the influence of foreign nongovernmental organizations as undermining the integrity of Tajikistan, singling out the Soros Foundation's Open Society Institute.[8] In the case of Uzbekistan (and possibly Turkmenistan), the most striking differences with Kyrgyzstan are the lack of secular domestic opposition and the greater ability and willingness to bring economic and military resources to bear, as evidenced by the Andijon crackdown of May 2005.

One point of disagreement among analysts is whether Kazakhstan's strong economic growth will gradually raise incomes in the region or will simply divide Central Asia into a wealthy north and an impoverished and isolated south. Kazakhstan has posted impressive economic growth figures for several years and will become a second-tier supplier of oil to the world market and, with Turkmenistan, an important regional supplier of natural gas, as discussed in Chapter Three. However, the prospects for foreign investment in Central Asia in sectors other than energy and mining are dim.

Turkmenistan's political and economic development remains perhaps the most unpredictable of all of the post-Soviet Central Asian

---

[6] Olcott (2005).

[7] Economist Intelligence Unit (2005a).

[8] Economist Intelligence Unit (2005c).

states. Absent major changes in leadership, Turkmenistan will remain isolated and connected to the rest of the region primarily through natural gas and cotton transport routes. Although the dearth of publicly available analysis on Turkmenistan reinforces its image as an isolated regime with little effect on developments in the region as a whole, it may also indicate practical constraints on access to the region facing analysts. It is notable that Turkmenistan's natural gas wealth has been instrumental in maintaining social stability through broad public subsidies. Turkmenistan may merit additional scrutiny if it becomes more closely integrated with south Asia and Iran as it pursues alternative export markets for its natural gas.

Uzbekistan will be pivotal to long-term developments in the region. Uzbekistan's trade and border policies will be crucial for Tajikistan's and Kyrgystan's economies, and its financial sector reform may determine whether Kazakhstan's considerable financial resources can be directed toward the rest of Central Asia, as discussed in Chapter Three. Even if Uzbekistan becomes increasingly marginalized in the economic future of the region, a failed Uzbekistan would invariably have important regional consequences, including increased refugee flows,[9] militarization of southern Kazakhstan and Turkmenistan, and potential political and economic restrictions in all the neighboring states. As a result, prevention of this outcome may be central to Central Asian and broader U.S. policy goals in the region.[10]

Before the events in Andijon, the conventional wisdom was that Uzbek power structures would be able to manage a stagnant economy, so long as export revenues did not collapse from a sustained and deep drop in commodity prices.[11] However, recent events have raised

---

[9] For example, Kyrgyzstan received hundreds of refugees in Osh and Jalalabad in the wake of the Andijon unrest in May 2005. The presence of a significant Uzbek minority in Kyrgyzstan (14 percent) and Tajikistan (25 percent), particularly in the Ferghana Valley, may affect the internal and regional relationships in case of a larger population displacement from Uzbekistan.

[10] "Uzbekistan: The Key to Success in Central Asia?" (2004).

[11] This point of view is articulated by a senior economist in Central Asia: "[Uzbekistan] is not coming apart, but it is also not going anywhere. The power structure in Uzbekistan has to realize this. Suharto's people understood this, that there was a bigger economic pie to be

questions about the nature and scope of domestic threats to the regime and about the extent to which economic frustration and political repression have emboldened domestic opposition and radical elements within the country. After the government crackdown on protestors in Andijon in May 2005, many observers in the diplomatic and business communities see Uzbekistan at a transition or tipping point, but they differ greatly on the range of possible outcomes.

The pace and nature of economic reform in Uzbekistan may directly affect these outcomes. However, President Karimov faces a formidable challenge in implementing genuine domestic reform with a weak institutional environment, divided leadership, and an increasingly frustrated population. If this reform effort is delayed or otherwise fails, the Uzbek leadership may face additional protests beyond the control of its security apparatus. A growing militant Islamic or insurgent movement may challenge the viability of the regime, reminiscent of the civil war in Tajikistan in the early 1990s or of post-Hussein Iraq.[12] Another possibility is a "Romanian" scenario,[13] where elements within the government depose Karimov to quell unrest.[14] However, for the time being, Uzbekistan has found some measure of stability through its growing relationships with Russia and China.

The challenge for the United States and the international community is finding effective policy tools to shape these outcomes or to hedge against them. The following sections analyze the role of assistance in the region and draw policy conclusions for the United States.

---

gotten by liberalizing the economy and this is better than just having a large share of a smaller pie. A collapse of Uzbekistan is not realistic. It would take a dramatic decline in cotton prices. The macroeconomic situation is not a big threat now."

[12] This point of view is articulated by a senior diplomat in Central Asia: "The disparity in incomes will grow exponentially between Uzbekistan and its neighbors. This can continue about five to seven years, and then an Islamic revolution may occur if there are no political reforms. Then we will have another Iran."

[13] Olcott (2005b).

[14] Karimov's older daughter, Gulnara, has an Interpol warrant out for her arrest as a result of a child-custody battle with a U.S. citizen, which could constrain not only her travel options but also her father's exit strategies.

Overview of Foreign Assistance in Central Asia

The prevailing wisdom since the collapse of the Soviet Union has been that the presence of western political and economic entities would have a beneficial effect on democratization and economic reform. However, the record of international financial institutions, multinational corporations, and international nongovernmental organizations has been decidedly mixed in Central Asia and particularly discouraging in Uzbekistan and Turkmenistan.[15] One challenge for the United States and the international community is to offer sound policies despite the opaqueness of the internal dynamics of the regimes in the region.

Total development assistance from both bilateral and multilateral sources to post-Soviet Central Asia amounted to more than $7 billion between 1992 and 2003, as shown in Figure A.1. One-third of this aid went to Kyrgyzstan, the "donors' darling" of Central Asia, making it by far the largest recipient of foreign aid in both absolute and per capita terms, as illustrated in Figure A.2. Approximately one-half of Tajikistan's foreign aid was allocated for humanitarian assistance after the civil wars of the 1990s. Turkmenistan, meanwhile, was largely ignored by western nations and the international donor community on account of its near absence of political and economic reform, poor record on human rights, and ability to generate income from natural gas exports to Russia and Ukraine.

Multilateral institutions have been the largest source of aid to Central Asia, accounting for more than one-third of the total aid flows to the region, as shown in Figure A.3. However, contributions from multilateral donors steadily decreased from 1998 to 2003, in part because of Kazakhstan's growing economy and the delays in economic reform in Uzbekistan. The United States and Japan have been the largest bilateral donors, each contributing about one-fifth of total aid to the region. U.S. bilateral contributions have steadily increased since 1998, reaching a peak in 2002, largely as a result of increasing commitment in the region after September 11, 2001.

---

[15] Cooley (2003).

Between 1992 and 2002, Central Asia was the "neglected child"[16] of the U.S. assistance program to the former Soviet Union, receiving only 12 percent of the total cumulative foreign aid budgeted to that region. A large portion of U.S. assistance in the region over the past decade went to humanitarian relief in war-torn Tajikistan and Kyrgyzstan and market reform in Kyrgyzstan and Kazakhstan, as shown in Figure 5.1.[17] Before Operation Enduring Freedom, U.S. security assistance was focused on safeguarding and remediating Kazakhstan's weapons of mass destruction infrastructure[18] as well as on developing low-level military relationships with Uzbekistan and Kyrgyzstan.

The events of September 11, 2001, led to a sea change in U.S. interests in the region, as Uzbekistan, Kyrgyzstan, and Turkmenistan became staging areas for military operations in Afghanistan. U.S. government aid temporarily shifted toward Uzbekistan, which received the largest increase in funding for 2002 in both absolute and percentage terms, as illustrated in Figure A.2.[19] In particular, the shift in security-related aid to Uzbekistan had elicited concern regarding U.S. support of Central Asian regimes with poor human-rights records and the perception of the United States as a regime guarantor.[20] However,

---

[16] Tarnoff (2002).

[17] The United States also has trade and investment programs through the Trade and Development Agency, Export-Import Bank (Eximbank), and Overseas Private Investment Corporation (OPIC). In addition to bilateral and regional aid, the United States plays a major role in international financial institutions operating in Central Asia, such as the IMF, the World Bank, and the Asian Development Bank.

[18] These efforts include safeguarding and mothballing the Aktau fast breeder reactor, eliminating biological and nuclear weapons infrastructure, and remediating biological and chemical toxins in the Aral Sea area.

[19] Although budgeted assistance to the region has decreased since 2002 in absolute terms, the projected fiscal year (FY) 2004 value is still approximately double (27 percent) the historical percentage (13 percent) of former Soviet aid given to Central Asia.

[20] For example, a Senate amendment to H.R. 2506 requires that the U.S. Secretary of State report biannually on defense assistance to Uzbekistan and give an accounting of human-rights violations. However, the language covering the human-rights reporting requirement was not included in the statement of conferees. See http://thomas.loc.gov/cgi-bin/bdquery/D?d107:45:./temp/~bd2Hd4::|TOM:/bss/d107query.html.

after the U.S. commitment in Iraq, aid to post-Soviet Central Asia in 2003 and 2004 decreased to near pre-September 11, 2001, levels. In July 2004, The U.S. State Department denied Uzbekistan certification to receive $18 million in aid for 2004, citing a lack of progress on democratic reform as outlined in their 2002 Strategic Partnership Framework. The crackdown on protesters in the Andijon region in May 2005 has further changed the dynamics of the Uzbek relationship with the United States and the international community. In July 2005, Uzbekistan officially evicted the United States from the Karshi-Khanabad air base. Although no official reason was given, it was widely assumed that the U.S. role in pressuring Kyrgyzstan not to return refugees from the events in Andijon back to Uzbekistan played a role in this decision. The U.S. military withdrew its last troops from the Karshi-Khanabad base in November 2005.

Figure 5.1
Cumulative U.S. Government Assistance to Central Asian Republics (FY 1992–FY 2002)

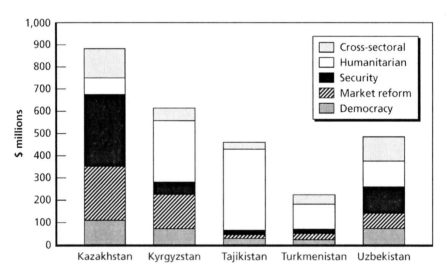

SOURCE: Nichol (2002).
RAND *MG417-5.1*

The effect of foreign aid on security and development is still a major topic of debate in both academic and policy circles. However, on balance, several broad conclusions can be drawn, with important implications for Central Asia.

For the past decade, a large number of governments, international financial institutions, and nongovernmental organizations have offered economic, social, and military assistance to the region, with mixed results. If one goal of international assistance is to help a country eventually access the international private capital market, Kazakhstan can be regarded as a success. Today, Kazakhstan has access to international financial markets, enjoys fairly well developed domestic financial markets and institutions, and has posted impressive economic growth figures over the past several years.[21] Donors have helped Kyrgyzstan and Tajikistan avert possible humanitarian crises and, some would argue, implement preliminary democratic and market reforms. However, both are expected to remain highly dependent on foreign aid and a very limited slate of export commodities.[22] The international community has had very little success in promoting economic or political reform in Uzbekistan and Turkmenistan and may, in fact, have inadvertently delayed it by lending to them in the 1990s.

There is evidence that foreign development assistance seldom becomes a reliable instrument of economic and social change unless a recipient country has good governance and also plays a willing role in formulating its own development strategy with the help of the donor community.[23] The poor record of Uzbekistan and Turkmenistan on both accounts is not encouraging. For countries with poor governance, foreign aid may be helpful in some cases if directed toward hu-

---

[21] Over the last few years, Kazakhstan has had stable and positive sovereign credit ratings from all major rating agencies including Standard and Poor's (BBB), Moody's (Baa3), and Fitch (BBB–). Several Kazakh banks, such as Xalyk Bank, Kazkommerzbank, Bank Alliance, and others, also have stable and positive credit ratings from major rating agencies.

[22] Economist in Central Asia: "The hidden message for Kyrgyzstan and Tajikistan is: You're a small country, you need to do everything well, and even then it will be tough."

[23] Akramov (forthcoming).

man capital creation, the promotion of civil society and governance, or directed assistance to the poor. The international community has largely pursued a policy of low-level engagement in Turkmenistan and Uzbekistan, which is consistent with these concerns.

Although the concept of aid coordination has been a theme in international aid circles over the past four decades, donor assistance for Central Asia is coordinated very loosely. Furthermore, a decreasing percentage of total U.S. foreign assistance is allocated through multilateral institutions, dropping to 5 percent in 2004.[24] Currently, aid coordination in Central Asia has included highly publicized meetings and conferences to help generate consensus on overarching regional policy issues. However, these events have largely been symbolic and have not generated meaningful cooperation among the countries of the region in dealing with (1) water and energy resources, (2) transportation infrastructure, (3) trade and investment, and (4) law enforcement and security.

Some have argued that only a massive infusion of coordinated international aid during the early 1990s might have averted the political and economic splintering of post-Soviet Central Asia. Despite repeated attempts at regional integration and overlapping regional initiatives, personal rivalries among the leaders in Central Asia have prevented cooperation on major transnational issues. The carrots and sticks available to the international aid community today may have only a limited effect on regimes that are increasingly sophisticated in diversifying their economic and security relationships in the region. Some have argued that low-level engagement and a "nuanced" approach are necessary in dealing with the authoritarian regimes in the region, otherwise access and influence will be ceded to other players, such as Russia, China, and Iran.

---

[24] Woods (2005).

Implications for the U.S. Role in Central Asia

As the United States clarifies its military relationships and commitments in Central Asia, it must consider the region's economic development itself as a long-term security concern. However, fundamental tradeoffs remain in the U.S. policy goals, which include near-term access to military bases in the region, long-term political and economic liberalization, regional stability, access to energy resources, and reducing the flow of narcotics to the world market. Several issues merit attention in the discussion of economic dimensions of security in Central Asia:

- Central Asia will increasingly diversify its economic and military relationships with neighbors such as Russia, China, and Iran, potentially crowding out U.S. influence in the region. The United States does not have a direct, compelling economic interest in Central Asia outside Kazakhstan's oil sector. Nor does most of Central Asia depend on direct economic assistance from or trade with the United States. Thus, Central Asia's economic future lies primarily within its own neighborhood. However, U.S. actions may have an effect on shaping the involvement of Central Asia's neighbors in the region. Insofar as the other regional powers share the U.S. goals of fostering development in the region, they should be engaged. In particular, cooperation with Russia may be crucial.
- Regime change in the region may occur with little warning and in spite of the efforts of the United States. If U.S. policymakers decide to maintain a military presence there, it may be necessary to consider a wider range of approaches that lower the risk of long-term denial of access and perceptions of the United States as a regime patron. Although some have argued that a U.S. military presence could be used as a vehicle for encouraging domestic reform, the record to date provides little grounds for opti-

mism. At a minimum, a lower-profile presence and hedging strategies should be part of U.S. strategic planning.[25]

- A "nuanced" approach may be necessary to deal with the more authoritarian regimes in Central Asia. The reality of governance in the region is that domestic policies are often the outcome of complex interactions among the elite stakeholders within the regime rather than of a centralized decision process. Although human-rights concerns may test the U.S. goal of promoting foreign policy at the intersection of our "vital interest and deepest beliefs," disengagement from Central Asia may compromise U.S. ability to attain overarching goals in the region. Policymakers should consider the costs and benefits of engaging alternative power centers within and outside of these regimes, possibly enlisting the support of other regional powers where common ground can be found.

- Economic and military assistance to the region should be more sharply focused to avoid the highest risk outcomes. In particular, failed state scenarios for Uzbekistan would result in major regional problems that would undermine broader U.S. goals, such as counterterror and counternarcotics strategies. However, policies that may be critical to stability, such as agricultural reform and free trade, remain important domestic political decisions and thus beyond the direct influence of the United States or multilateral institutions. Although a portfolio approach to international assistance in the region has merit, a greater focus of diplomatic capital and economic resources on specific issues, such as political liberalization, may be necessary.

In conclusion, economic development will be crucial to the future of Central Asia and broader U.S. interests in the region. Although there are indications that the states of the region recognize this, it is unclear whether they have the institutional capacity to implement sound and lasting economic policies and whether the United

---

[25] For a perspective on the U.S. military role in the region, please refer to Oliker and Shlapak (2005).

States and the international community are offering the appropriate combination of incentives to enable this. The United States has limited ability or interest in becoming a regime patron but still may play a significant role in shaping the prospects for development in the region by influencing the nature and pace of political and economic reform, realizing that the principles and interests behind U.S. involvement are more enduring than any single regime is likely to be.

U.S. and International Assistance to Central Asia Before and After 9/11

Figure A.1
Development Assistance to Central Asian Republics (1992–2003)

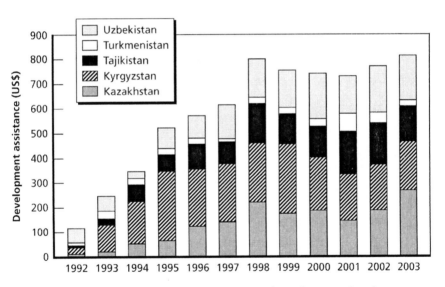

SOURCE: Organization for Economic Cooperation and Development, Development Assistance Committee, "International Development Statistics."
RAND MG417-A.1

Figure A.2
Distribution of Cumulative Development Assistance Among Central Asian
Republics (1992–2003)

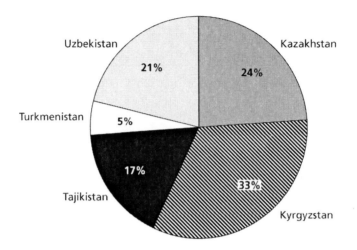

SOURCE: Organization for Economic Cooperation and Development, Development
Assistance Committee, "International Development Statistics."
RAND MG417-A.2

Figure A.3
Sources of Development Assistance to Central Asian Republics

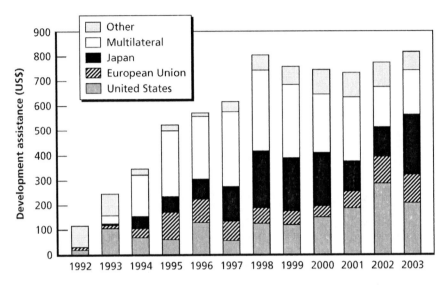

SOURCE: Organization for Economic Cooperation and Development, Development
Assistance Committee, "International Development Statistics."
RAND *MG417-A.3*

Figure A.4
Sources of Cumulative Development Assistance to Central Asian Republics
(1992–2003)

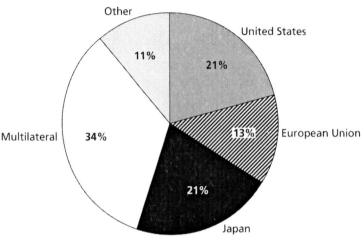

RAND *MG417-A.4*

Table A.1
Cumulative International Financial Institution Credits to Central Asian
Republics (1991–2004)

IFI	Kazakhstan	Kyrgyzstan	Tajikistan	Uzbekistan
IMF (million SDR)[a]	445.5	251.4	153.7	165.2
World Bank (US$ million)				
Commitments	1,925	649	333	599
Disbursements	1,456	479	244	268
European Bank for Reconstruction and Development (million Euro)	>1,000	151	32	528
Asian Development Bank (US$ million)	501.6	532.7	210.9	794.7

SOURCES: International Monetary Fund, World Bank; European Bank for
Reconstruction and Development; and Asian Development Bank.

NOTE: Turkmenistan is not included in the table because it has not received a
significant amount of credit from any IFI.

[a] A Special Drawing Right (SDR) is a unit of account used by the IMF based on a
basket of international currencies. The exchange rate as of May 27, 2005, was 1.485
US$ for one SDR. See http://www.imf.org/external/np/exr/facts/sdr.htm.

Table A.2
U.S. Government Assistance to Central Asian Republics (1994–2003)
(US$ million)

Country	1994	1995	1996	1997	1998	1999	2000	2001	2002	2003	1994–2003
Kazakhstan	**106.6**	**41.6**	**30.3**	**11.7**	**38.1**	**50.6**	**53.4**	**68.2**	**80.5**	**60.3**	**541.3**
Economic	106.5	41.5	29.9	9.8	35.3	48.3	51.3	46.7	54.3	45.2	468.8
Military	0.1	0.1	0.4	1.9	2.8	2.3	2.1	21.5	26.2	15.1	72.5
Kyrgyzstan	**68.3**	**50.7**	**40.3**	**24.4**	**38.5**	**52.9**	**47.3**	**37**	**77.6**	**58.6**	**495.6**
Economic	68.2	50.6	40.1	23.3	36.8	51	45.9	34.7	65.9	51.1	467.6
Military	0.1	0.1	0.2	1.1	1.7	1.9	1.4	2.3	11.7	7.5	28
Tajikistan	**65.2**	**39.6**	**21.3**	**23.8**	**33.9**	**38.4**	**36.1**	**62.4**	**89.1**	**52.3**	**462.1**
Economic	65.2	39.6	21.3	23.8	33.9	38.4	36.1	62.4	77.6	51	449.3
Military	0	0	0	0	0	0	0	0	11.5	1.3	12.8
Turkmenistan	**28**	**5.4**	**29.2**	**3.8**	**6.3**	**13.2**	**9.3**	**9.7**	**18.9**	**7.8**	**131.6**
Economic	27.9	5.3	29	3	5.5	12.3	8.4	8.6	11.4	6.8	118.2
Military	0.1	0.1	0.2	0.8	0.8	0.9	0.9	1.1	7.5	1	13.4
Uzbekistan	**24.5**	**11.7**	**11.2**	**5.7**	**15.8**	**35.8**	**34**	**57.1**	**170.2**	**75.2**	**441.2**
Economic	24.5	11.6	10.9	4.4	13.8	33.6	31.7	48.9	125.1	61.6	366.1
Military	0	0.1	0.3	1.3	2	2.2	2.3	8.2	45.1	13.6	75.1
Total	**292.6**	**149**	**132.3**	**69.4**	**132.6**	**190.9**	**180.1**	**234.4**	**436.3**	**254.2**	**2071.8**
Economic	292.3	148.6	131.2	64.3	125.3	183.6	173.4	201.3	334.3	215.7	1870
Military	0.3	0.4	1.1	5.1	7.3	7.3	6.7	33.1	102	38.5	201.8

Bibliography

Abdullayev, Zafar, "Tajikistan's Capital Amnesty Barely Dents Shadow Economy," Eurasianet.org, June 23, 2003. Online at http://www.eurasianet.org/departments/business/articles/eav062303.shtml.

Aghion, P., and P. Bolton, "Distribution and Growth in Models of Imperfect Capital Markets," *European Economic Review*, Vol. 36, 1992, pp. 603–611.

Akramov, Kamiljon, "Governance and Foreign Aid Allocation," Santa Monica, Calif.: Pardee RAND Graduate School, forthcoming.

Alesina A., and D. Rodrik, "Distributive Politics and Economic Growth," *Quarterly Journal of Economics*, Vol. 109, 1994, pp. 465–490.

". . . And Criticizes Turkmenistan's Lack of Cooperation," *Radio Free Europe/Radio Liberty Newsline*, Vol. 8, No. 42, Part I, March 4, 2004.

Asian Development Bank, *Asian Development Outlook*, Hong Kong, updated 2004.

———, *Key Indicators*, Hong Kong, 2005.

Babakulov, Ulugbek, et al., "Investigation: Kyrgyz 'Slaves' on Kazakh Plantations," *Institute for War and Peace Reporting*, September 11, 2003. Online at http://www.iwpr.net/index.pl?archive/rca/rca_200308_222_1_eng.txt.

Baldauf, Scott, and Laura J. Winter, "Kashmir Prized But Little Aided: Separatists and Mosques Filled in the Void of Official Quake *Aid*," *Christian Science Monitor*, October 14, 2005.

Birdsall N., D. Ross, and R. Sabot, "Inequality and Growth Reconsidered: Lessons from East Asia," *World Bank Economic Review*, Vol. 9, No. 3, 1995, pp. 477–508.

Bohr, Annette, "Regionalism in Central Asia: New Geopolitics, Old Regional Order," *International Affairs,* Vol. 80, No. 3, May 2004.

BP Statistical Review of World Energy, June 2005.

Buchan, David, "Chubais Suggests East-West Electricity Power Grid," *Financial Times*, March 28, 2002.

Central Intelligence Agency, *The World Factbook, 2005.* Online at http://www.cia.gov/cia/publications/factbook/.

Chebotarayov, Andrei, "Kazakhstan: Corruption Boosts Economy," *Institute for War and Peace Reporting*, August 20, 2003. Online at http://www.iwpr.net/index.pl?archive/rca/rca_200308_227_3_eng.txt.

"ChevronTexaco Subpoenaed on Kazakhstan," *Reuters*, September 11, 2003.

Chevron-Texaco website, 2002. Online at http://www.chevrontexaco.com/news/press/2002/2002-03-20.asp.

Clarke, G.R.G., "More Evidence on Income Distribution and Growth," *Journal of Development Economics*, Vol. 47, 1995, pp. 403–427.

Cooley, Alexander, "Western Conditions and Domestic Choices: The Influence of External Actors on the Post-Communist Transition," in Adrian Karatnycky, Alexander Motyl, and Amanda Schnetzer (eds.), *Nations in Transition 2003: Democratization in East Center Europe and Eurasia,* Washington, D.C.: Freedom House, 2003.

———, "Depoliticizing Manas: The Domestic Consequences of the U.S. Military Presence in Kyrgyzstan," PONARS Policy Memo 362, Washington, D.C., February 2005.

Deininger K., and L. Squire, "A New Dataset Measuring Income Inequality," *World Bank Economic Review*, Vol. 10, No. 3, 1996, pp. 565–591.

———, "New Ways of Looking at Old Issues: Inequality and Growth," *Journal of Development Economics*, Vol. 57, 1998, pp. 259–287.

Dejevsky, Mary, *The Independent*, January 7, 2004. Online at http://news.independent.co.uk/world/asia/story.jsp?story=478642.

De Nicoló, Gianni, et al., "Financial Development in the CIS-7 Countries: Bridging the Great Divide," European Bank for Reconstruction and Development, IMF Working Paper, WP/03/205, Washington, D.C., 2003.

Economist Intelligence Unit, *Country Report: Tajikistan*, New York, June 2003a.

———, *Country Report, Uzbekistan*, New York, June 2003b,

———, *Country Report, Turkmenistan,* New York, 2003c.

———, *Country Report, Kazakhstan*, New York, April 2005a.

———, *Country Report, Kyrgyzstan*, New York, May 2005b.

———, *Country Report, Tajikistan*, New York, March 2005c.

———, *Country Report, Turkmenistan*, New York, April 2005d.

———, *Country Report, Ubekistan*, New York, 2005e.

Eilat, Yair, and Clifford Zinnes, "The Shadow Economy in Transition Countries: Consequences for Economic Growth and Donor Assistance," CAER II Discussion Paper No. 83, Harvard Institute for International Development, September 2000, online at http://www.cid.harvard.edu/caer2/htm/content/papers/paper83/paper83.pdf.

Energy Information Administration, "Iran Country Analysis Brief," Washington, D.C., March 2005a.

———, "Iraq Country Analysis Brief," Washington, D.C., June 2005b.

European Bank for Reconstruction and Development, *Transition Report 2002*, London, November 2002.

———, "Strategy for Uzbekistan," London, March 4, 2003, p. 16.

———, *Country Strategies*, London, 2005.

Figini, Paolo, "Inequality and Growth Revisited," Trinity Economic Paper Series, Paper No. 99/2, Dublin, Ireland, 1999.

Goncharov, Vyacheslav "Kyrgyzstan Struggles to Stem Smuggling," Eurasianet.org, August 5, 2003, online at http://www.eurasianet.org/departments/business/articles/eav080503_pr.shtml.

"Government Takes Steps to Prevent Human Trafficking," *UzReport*, September 29, 2003.

Helbling, Thomas, et al., "Debt accumulation in the CIS-7 Countries: Bad Luck, Bad Policies, or Bad Advice?" IMF Working Paper, WP/04/93, Washington, D.C., 2004.

Hill, Fiona, "Eurasia on the Move: The Regional Implications of Mass Labor Migration from Central Asia to Russia," Presentation at The Kennan Institute, Washington, D.C., September 27, 2004, online at http://www.brook.edu/scholars/fhill.htm.

Hill, Fiona, and Regine Spector, *The Caspian Basin and Asian Energy Markets*, Conference Report No. 8, The Brookings Institution, Washington, D.C., September 2001.

Institute for War and Peace Reporting website, online at http://www.iwpr.net/index.pl?archive/rca/rca_200308_224_1_eng.txt.

International Crisis Group, "Incubators of Conflict: Central Asia's Localized Poverty and Social Unrest," Asia Report No. 16, Osh/Brussels, June 8, 2001a.

———, "Central Asia: Drugs and Conflict," Asia Report No. 25, Osh/Brussels, November 26, 2001b.

———, *Cracks in the Marble: Turkmenistan's Failing Dictatorship*, Osh/Brussels, January 17, 2003a.

———, *Tajikistan: A Roadmap for Development*, Osh/Brussels, April 2003b, p. 19.

———, *Tajikistan: Poor and Getting Poorer Despite Aid Efforts*, Osh/Brussels, April 24, 2003c.

International Monetary Fund Press Release No. 03/188, November 11, 2003.

International Organization on Migration website. Online at http://www.iom.int.

"Justice Department Subpoenas ChevronTexaco," *Associated Press*, September 11, 2003.

Karasik, Theodore, "Medical NGOs and Health Service Implications: Islamic Insurgents in the Caucasus and Central Asia," unpublished RAND research, September 2001.

Karasik, Theodore, "Central Asian Traditional Medicine," in *Encyclopedia of Modern Asia*, Great Barrington, Mass.: Berkshire Publications, 2002.

Karasik, Theodore, and George Allen, "Grozny and Beyond: Health Service Implications of Urban Combat," unpublished RAND research, February 2002.

"Kazakhstan Begins Process of Legalizing Shadow Economy," *Radio Free Europe/Radio Liberty News*, June 30, 2003.

Kazi, Aftab, "Is the Proposed Russia-China-India Pipeline Feasible?" *Central Asia-Caucasus Analyst*, January 13, 2003. Online at http://www.cacianalyst.org/view_article.php?articleid=378.

Kholmuradov, Kamol, "Farmers Express Discontent in Uzbekistan, Despite Projected Record Wheat Crop," Eurasianet.org, July 29, 2003.

Klitgaard, Robert, and Heather Baser, "Working Together to Fight Corruption: State, Society and the Private Sector in Partnership," in Suzanne Taschereau and Jose Edgardo L. Campos, eds., *Governance Innovations: Lessons from Experience, Building Government-Citizen-Business Partnerships*, Canada: Institute on Governance, 1997.

Ledeneva, Alena, "Commonwealth of Independent States," *Global Corruption Report 2003*, Transparency International, 2003, p. 165.

Lia, Brynar, and Ashlid Kjok, "Energy Supply as Terrorist Targets? Patterns of Petroleum Terrorism: 1968-1999," in Daniel Heradstveit and Helge Hveem, eds., *Oil in the Gulf: Obstacles to Democracy and Development*, Aldershot, Hampshire, United Kingdom: Asghate, 2004.

"Lure of the West," *The Economist*, June 14, 2001.

Makarenko, Tamara, "Terrorist Threat to Energy and Infrastructure Increases," *Jane's Intelligence Review*, June 2003.

Marat, Erica, "Kyrgyzstan Adopts Georgian Model to Fight Corruption," *Eurasia Daily Monitor*, June 7, 2005. Online at http://jamestown.org/edm/article.php?article_id=2369842.

Marsh, Peter, "Kazakhstan Seeks to Attract Foreign Investors to Boost Nuclear Energy Research," *Financial Times*, June 17, 2003, p. 6.

Micklin, Philip, *Managing Water in Central Asia*, London: The Royal Institute of International Affairs, 2000.

Najibullah, Farangis, "Central Asia: Tajikistan, Kyrgyzstan Making Efforts to Reform Health Care Systems," *RFE/RFL*, March 27, 2003. Online at http://www.rferl.org/nca/features/2003/03/27032003180714.asp.

Nichol, Jim, "Central Asia's New States: Political Developments and Implications for U.S. Interests," *Issue Brief for Congress*, November 7, 2002.

———, "Central Asia's New States: Political Developments and Implications for U.S. Interests," *Issue Brief for Congress*, updated April 1, 2003.

"Nigeria, Colombia Pipeline Deaths Mounting," *Oil & Gas Journal Online*, October 26, 1998.

Olcott, Martha Brill, "International Gas Trade in Central Asia: Turkmenistan, Iran, Russia, and Afghanistan," Geopolitics of Gas Working Paper Series, Stanford University, Stanford, California, May 2004.

———, "Uzbekistan's Tipping Point: The Violence in Andijan and What Comes Next," United States Helsinki Commission Briefing on Uzbekistan, Washington, D.C., May 19, 2005.

———, "In Uzbekistan, the Revolution Won't Be Pretty," *Washington Post*, May 22, 2005.

Oliker, Olga, and Thomas S. Szayna, eds., *Faultlines of Conflict in Central Asia and the South Caucasus: Implications for the U.S. Army*, Santa Monica, Calif.: RAND Corporation, MR-1598-A, 2003.

Oliker, Olga, and David A. Shlapak, *U.S. Interests in Central Asia: Policy Priorities and Military Roles*, Santa Monica, Calif.: RAND Corporation, MG-338-AF, 2005.

On the Implementation of the Program on Counteracting the AIDS Epidemic in the Republic of Kazakhstan for 2001–2002: Material of the Meeting of Representatives of President of Kazakhstan Administration, Ministries, Agencies, and Local Executive Authority Bodies, Astana, Kazakhstan, October 20, 2001.

Organization for Economic Cooperation and Development, "International Development Statistics." Online at www.oecd.org/dac/stats/idsonline.

Orhant, Melanie, "Stop-Traffic Moderator, Human Trafficking—Regional Profile 2003-03-11," 2003. Online at http://www.unodc.un.or.th/material/document/RegionalProfile.pdf.

Overview of SME Sector in the Republic of Uzbekistan, Swiss-IFC Central Asia Partnership Program, Tashkent, 2002.

Peak, Maitland J. "Aaron," "Summary of Fact Finding Mission to Kazakhstan," 2001. Online at http://www.eurasianet.org/policy_forum/kazakhst030101.

"Platts Guide to the Caspian," accessed 2003. Online at http://www.platts.com/features/caspian/pipeline.shtml.

Population, Health and Nutrition Information Project, "Turkmenistan," Washington, D.C., March 2002.

Program of Counteraction to HIV/AIDS Epidemic in the Armed Forces of the Republic of Kazakhstan for 2002–2005, Astana, Kazakhstan, 2002, pp. 40–63.

Program on Counteracting the AIDS Epidemic in the Republic of Kazakhstan for 2001–2005, Approved by the Resolution of the Government of the Republic of Kazakhstan, No. 1207, September 14, 2001, pp. 116–160.

RAO-UES Press Release, 22 September 2004. Online at http://www.rao-ees.ru/en.

Report of the International Narcotics Board Control, 2002. Online at http://www.incb.org/e/ar/2002/.

"Report Says Children Harvest 40 Percent of Tajik Cotton," *RFE/RL Newsline,* Vol. 8, No. 136, Part I, July 20, 2004.

Ruban, Olga, interview with General Andrey Nikolayev, "The Borderless Expanses of the Fatherland. General Andrey Nikolayev Proposes to Organize the Borders with the CIS Countries Based Upon the Zipper Principle: So That They Can Be Easily Opened and Closed," Ekspert (Moscow), December 17, 2001.

Rumer, Boris, and Stanislaw Zhukov, "Broader Parameters: Development in the Twentieth Century," in Boris Rumer and Stanislaw Zhukov, eds., *Central Asia: The Challenges of Independence,* Delhi, India: Aakar Books, 2003, p. 64.

"Russia to Gain Control of Tajik Power Station," *RFE/RL Newsline,* Vol. 8, No. 164, Part I, August 27, 2004.

Schwartz, Stephen, "Getting Uzbekistan Wrong," *The Weekly Standard,* May 16, 2005.

Sevastopulo, Demetri, and Hubert Wetzel, "Pentagon Resists Air Base Cash Demands," *Financial Times,* October 29, 2005.

Startseva, Alla, "UES Looking to Move into Ex-USSR Power," *The St. Petersburg Times,* September 9, 2003a. Online at http://www.times.spb.ru/archive/times/900/news/b_10231.htm.

————, "EU and Russia Agree on Grid Integration," *The St. Petersburg Times*, October 17, 2003b. Online at http://www.times.spb.ru/archive/times/911/news/b_10662.htm.

Stone, Peter H., "Patton Boggs Flacks for Kazakhstan," *National Journal*, September 17, 2003. Online at www.eurasia.org.ru.

Strategic Program of Response to HIV/AIDS Epidemic within Ministry of Education and Science of the Republic of Kazakhstan for 2002–2005, Astana, Kazakhstan, 2002, pp. 57–76.

Sulaimanova, Sultanat, "Migration Trends in Central Asia and the Case of Trafficking of Women," in Dan Burghart and Theresa Sabonis-Helf, eds., *In the Tracks of Tamerlane: Central Asia's Path to the 21st Century*, Chapter 18, Washington, D.C.: National Defense University Press, 2004.

Swiss-IFC Central Asia Partnership Program, *Business Environment in Uzbekistan*, Tashkent, 2002.

Tarnoff, Curt, "The Former Soviet Union and U.S. Foreign Assistance," *Issue Brief for Congress*, updated May 20, 2002.

Taube, Gunther, and Jeromin Zettelmeyer, "Output Declines and Recovery in Uzbekistan—Past Performance and Future Prospects," IMF working paper, WP 98/132, Washington, D.C., 1998.

Templer, Robert, "Tough Lines in Central Asia," in *Global Corruption Report 2003*, Transparency International, 2003, p. 166.

Torbakov, Igor, "Russia Seeks to Use Energy Abundance to Increase Political Leverage," Eurasianet.org, November 19, 2003. Online at http://www.eurasianet.org/departments/insight/articles/eav111903_pr.shtml.

Tracy, Jen, "Case Study 6: Mobilizing Resources for Health, The First Phase of Kyrgyzstan's Co-Payment Policy," in Erio Ziglio et al., eds., *Health Systems Confront Poverty*, World Health Organization, Regional Office for Europe, Copenhagen, Denmark, 2003.

Transparency International, 2004. Online at http://www.transparency.org/pressreleases_archive/2004/2004.10.20.cpi.en.html.

"Turkmenistan Turns Down Invitation to Join CIS Power System," *RFE/RL Newsline*, Vol. 8., No. 28, Part 1, February 12, 2004.

"UNAIDS Assisted Response to HIV/AIDS, STIs, and Drug Abuse in Central Asian Countries, 1996–2000," Almaty: UNAIDS, January 2001.

United Nations Conference on Trade and Development, *World Investment Report*, Annex B tables, 2004.

United Nations Development Programme, *Human Development Report 2002*, New York: Oxford University Press, 2002.

———, *Human Development Report 2003*, New York: Oxford University Press, 2003.

———, *Human Development Report 2004*, New York: Oxford University Press, 2004.

United Nations Information Service, "UN Launches Five Major Drug Control Projects in Central Asia," June 20, 2003. Online at http://usinfo.state.gov/regional/eur/eurasia/030620-drugcontrol.htm.

United Nations Office on Drug and Crime, *The Opium Economy in Afghanistan: An International Problem*, Vienna, 2003.

United Nations Population Fund. Online at http://www.unfpa.org/modules/6billion/populationissues/demographic.htm (accessed August 2005).

"U.S. Aid to Uzbekistan: Carrots and Sticks (Part 2)," *Radio Free Europe/Radio Liberty Central Asia Report*, Vol. 4, No. 29, July 2004.

U.S. Energy Information Administration, "World Proved Reserves of Oil and Natural Gas, Most Recent Estimates." Online at http://www.eia.doe.gov/emeu/international/reserves.html. (Original Source: PennWell Corporation, *Oil & Gas Journal*, Vol. 100, No. 52, December 23, 2002.)

"Uzbek President Hammers Minister over Unpaid Wages," *Radio Free Europe/Radio Liberty Central Asia Report*, Vol. 3, No. 30, September 5, 2003.

"Uzbekistan: The Key to Success in Central Asia?" Hearing Before the Subcommittee on the Middle East and Central Asia of the Committee on International Relations, U.S. House of Representatives, Washington, D.C., June 15, 2004.

Vahidy, Hassaan, and Fereidun Fesharaki, "Pakistan's Gas Discoveries Eliminate Import Need," *Oil and Gas Journal*, Vol. 100.4, June 28, 2002, pp. 24–34.

Wade, John, "Violence, Crime Continue to Cast Shadow Over Future Oil Investment in Colombia," *Oil & Gas Journal Online*, January 17, 2000.

Williams, Phil, "Criminalization and Stability in Central Asia and South Caucasus," in Olga Oliker and Thomas S. Szayna, eds., *Faultlines of Conflict in Central Asia and the South Caucasus: Implications for the U.S. Army*, Santa Monica, Calif.: RAND Corporation, MR-1598-A, 2003.

Wolf, Charles, Jr., K. C. Yeh, Benjamin Zycher, Nick Eberstadt, and Sung-Ho Lee, *Fault Lines in China's Economic Terrain*, Santa Monica, Calif.: RAND Corporation, MR-1686-NA/SRF, 2003.

Woods, Ngaire, "The Shifting Politics of Foreign Aid," *International Affairs*, Vol. 81, No. 2, 2005, pp. 393–409.

World Bank, *Making Transition Work for Everyone*, Washington, D.C., 2000.

———, "Shadow Economy Reserve for Growth," interview with Christof Ruehl, Chief Economist, Russia Country Office, November 11, 2002. Online at http://www.worldbank.org.ru/ECA/Russia.nsf/0/F5BB4A914304C9B9C3256CB600350661.

———, *Uzbekistan Living Standards Assessment: Policies to Improve Living Standards), Vol. 1: Summary Report,* and *Volume II: Full Report,* No. 25923-UZ, Washington, D.C., 2003a.

———, *Uzbekistan Report,* Washington, D.C., 2003b.

———, *Uzbekistan Living Standards Assessment: Aspects of Institutional Analysis, Health and Social Assistance Delivery*, Washington, D.C., 2003c.

———, *World Development Indicators 2004,* Washington, D.C., 2004.

———, *World Development Indicators 2005*, Washington, D.C., 2005a.

———, *Growth, Poverty, and Inequality: Eastern Europe and the Former Soviet Union,* Wasington, D.C., 2005b.

Yergin, Daniel, and Michael Stoppard, "The Next Prize," *Foreign Affairs*, Vol. 82, No. 6, 2003.

Yermukanov, Marat, "Kazakhstan's Rough Road to WTO Accession," *Eurasia Daily Monitor*, Vol. 1, Issue 78, September 3, 2004.

Zaslavski, Alexander, "Government Claims Success in Kazakhstan Capital Amnesty," July 23, 2001, Eurasianet. Online at http://www.eurasianet.org/departments/business/articles/eav072301.shtml.